T0209405

BASICS ABOUT
SALES, USE, AND OTHER
TRANSACTIONAL TAXES

BASICS ABOUT SALES, USE, AND OTHER TRANSACTIONAL TAXES

Overview of transactional taxes for consideration when striving toward the maximazation of tax compliance and minimazation of tax costs.

ESTHER E. CARRANZA

BASICS ABOUT SALES, USE, AND OTHER TRANSACTIONAL TAXES

Overview of transactional taxes for consideration when striving toward the maximazation of tax compliance and minimazation of tax costs.

iUniverse books may be ordered through booksellers or by contacting:

iUniverse
1663 Liberty Drive
Bloomington, IN 47403
www.iuniverse.com
844-349-9409

Because of the dynamic nature of the Internet, any web addresses or links contained in this book may have changed since publication and may no longer be valid. The views expressed in this work are solely those of the author and do not necessarily reflect the views of the publisher, and the publisher hereby disclaims any responsibility for them.

Any people depicted in stock imagery provided by Getty Images are models, and such images are being used for illustrative purposes only.
Certain stock imagery © Getty Images.

ISBN: 978-1-6632-4953-1 (sc)
ISBN: 978-1-6632-4936-4 (hc)
ISBN: 978-1-6632-4952-4 (e)

Library of Congress Control Number: 2023900462

Print information available on the last page.

iUniverse rev. date: 04/06/2023

Contents

Introduction

Throughout my career, I have found that people with different levels of education and business experience express some fear of sales taxes. The most common comment I have heard from these people is that taxes are too complicated and that they do not have the skills or knowledge to understand them. Surprisingly, this list of people includes CPAs, financial accountants, lawyers, business executives, middle management, and clerical personnel. Well, I disagree with all these people.

Anyone who is sufficiently interested and willing to open his or her mind can learn about and understand taxes. I know this for a fact. For more than forty years, I have taught and explained taxes to many individuals. Now, they may not be tax experts today, but they do understand enough to be more proficient in their job responsibilities and are more comfortable with, and better at, making decisions that involve transactional taxes.

If you are living in a civilized society, chances are quite high that either you have paid or will have to pay taxes, either directly or indirectly, on items or services that you acquire or possess. Taxes are imposed upon the majority of things that you buy, use, and/or possess. As it has been said, taxes are unavoidable.

Some people may not believe this, but taxes are important, contributing to the well-being of the society in which you live and to your personal well-being. But in order to understand, appreciate, and take advantage of some of the benefits of any tax, you will need to have a basic understanding of taxes, tax implementation, and tax application.

Basics about Sales, Use, and Other Transactional Taxes is intended to explain transactional taxes in layperson's language with the purpose of making it easier for the reader to understand and manage his or her transactional taxes and minimize tax-related costs. Transactional taxes are taxes that are imposed upon the value of items, goods, and services at the time of their sale, use, or storage. This includes taxes known as sales, use, value-added, goods and services, and excise taxes, which are imposed by authorized governments and entities.

Using the information shared herein should make it easier for you to understand and recognize how transactional taxes are involved with your business and personal transactions. It should also make it easier for you to understand how to avoid paying more taxes than you owe.

Basics about Sales, Use, and Other Transactional Taxes describes the different components of transactional taxes—its primary focus—that are imposed upon the sale, purchase, or bartering of items and services. It also focuses on consumption taxes, which are commonly known as use taxes, and provides information on taxes imposed upon international trade. This information should make it easier for you to understand transactional taxes and help you recognize when you need to ask for help from a tax expert, tax lawyer, or other tax professional.

Basics about Sales, Use, and Other Transactional Taxes also describes activities associated with the implementation, management, and remittance of these taxes, including elaboration on the regulatory agencies that enact the rules and regulations associated with taxes, descriptions of the different rules and regulations, and identification of applicable taxes and the method of collecting said taxes. Also addressed are responsibilities regarding the remittance of taxes, recordkeeping, and the reporting of taxes, and tax audits.

My goal is to share some basic understanding of transactional taxes in a manner that is easy for the reader to understand. With this in mind, *Basics about Sales, Use, and Other Transactional Taxes* seeks to do the following:

1) Describe transactional taxes in a nontechnical manner for easy reading.

2) Describe the basic principles and scope of transactional taxes.

3) Help the reader to understand transactional taxes sufficiently so he or she may perform the most basic of tax-related activities without the need to hire a professional tax expert.

4) Provide information that may be used to help identify and avoid the overpayment of transactional taxes.

5) Help identify activities one needs to complete to be compliant with tax laws and regulations.

6) Help the reader recognize when to request assistance from tax experts and/or lawyers.

Basics about Sales, Use, and Other Transactional Taxes is not intended to give professional advice. Instead, it is intended to share basic information about transactional taxes. It is also intended to help you, the reader, to decide when to seek advice from a tax professional or do more research and/or studying on the subject matter, that is, if you feel sufficiently comfortable to do so.

Chapter 1

Elements of Transactional Taxes

Taxpayers should keep in mind the different elements involved in transactional taxes. To address the basics of taxes, we should start with the purpose and goals of taxes. Some taxpayers consider some of the elements, such as understanding the related legislative processes, tax agencies and authorities, and the information shared among tax authorities, to be unimportant. However, all taxpayers should consider the responsibilities with taxes, tax reporting, and remittances to be very important. Some taxpayers will deal with each of these elements regularly, whereas others will deal with only some of them on an as-needed basis.

Taxes are implemented and used with two primary goals in mind: (1) to provide benefits to the society and the population from which they are collected and (2) to finance these benefits via government services. Most taxes are implemented to finance common government services including health care, public education, police, and environmental protection. Some taxes are implemented for very specific purposes and for a specific time period. In all cases, before a tax law is passed, its benefits to the society will be considered, and when the law is passed, its purpose, scope, and implementation will be described. The revenue derived from the different types of taxes enables the protection and support of the society and its population, along with enabling the financing of the tax agencies and the government(s) responsible for the management of these taxes.

Taxes are implemented by the legislative branch of a government via the enactment of laws and regulations. Through such enacted legislation, the rights and obligations associated with transactional taxes are also defined.

Tax enforcement and tax management is addressed from two perspectives: (1) governmental and (2) business. From the governmental perspective, the identification, collection, and disbursement of taxes is defined, enacted, and enforced by the governmental taxing authorities. Tax laws and regulations are levied at the federal, state, and local level of government. From the business perspective, agreements are made between two or more parties when negotiating a business transaction and may include terms and conditions relating to taxes in contracts, purchase orders, master agreements, etc. These tax-related terms and conditions usually elaborate upon the tax responsibilities that each of the participating parties have agreed upon. Most of these terms and conditions will likely be a reiteration of governmental tax laws and regulations. Some will likely identify the responsibility of each party to comply, and some will identify who is to be the direct payer of such costs. So, if any component of the terms and conditions of a contract is found to be noncompliant with applicable laws and regulations, it will likely be considered nonenforceable.

All buyers and sellers are affected by tax laws and any contracts that list tax-related terms and conditions. Because of this, it is wise to understand transactional taxes and how they affect you and your business.

TAXING AGENCIES AND AUTHORITIES

Different tiers of government are empowered to impose transactional taxes upon individuals, business entities, estates, trusts, and any other organization or person who is recognized by the taxing entity. This taxing power is based on the constitution of the respective governments.

Once a government entity enacts a transaction-related tax law or regulation, the imposition of said law or regulation is limited to the jurisdiction of that government entity and to the scope defined. That is, the taxing powers of the United States government, and any of its lower tiers, cannot impose taxes on jurisdictions outside its jurisdictional reach. Nor may another nation or any of its subdivisions impose taxes on activities or transactions that are completed within the jurisdiction of the United States or any of its subdivisions.

The imposition of tax laws flows downstream, upon the lower tiers of taxing jurisdictions. Each lower tier must adhere to the laws and regulations of the higher-tiered governments and with court rulings. Said in another way, the government of the United States can only impose taxes upon transactions that are completed inside the borders of the United States. Here, jurisdiction is at the federal level, making an impact on subdivisions such as states and territories and on the subdivisions of these tiers. Tax laws that are enacted by a state will affect transactions that are completed within that state's jurisdiction or borders, including its subdivisions, such as counties, parishes, or boroughs, and the subdivisions of those subdivisions. Taxes enacted by a county are limited to the county's jurisdiction; city taxes are limited to the city's jurisdiction; and so on.

But be aware that some local governments cannot impose taxes. In order to do so, the government must have prior authorization by the constitution of the state or the US Constitution.

Some government entities can and will create a special purpose district when needed. Generally, a special purpose district is created for a limited taxing purpose and/or a limited period of time. Sometimes, a special purpose district is also known as a special district government, special tax district, or special tax authority, board, or commission.

A special purpose district is designed to operate separately and independently from the government entity that authorizes it. Usually, it will have its own administrative staff to operate it and will be fiscally independent. A special purpose district will determine where and when the tax is to be imposed, what the tax rate will be, and how the revenue is to be spent.

It is also possible that two or more taxing entities may cooperate and create a special purpose district that applies to both their jurisdictions. An example is when more than two closely located cities and/or towns create a metropolitan transit authority.

Following are a few of the many special purpose districts and their respective jurisdictions:

San Antonio Metropolitan Transit Authority
Purpose: Provide transportation for the metropolitan area of San Antonio, Texas.

Participating municipalities include San Antonio, Alamo Heights, Bacones Heights, Castle Hill, and China Grove.

Houston Metropolitan Transit Authority
Purpose: Provide transportation for the metropolitan area of Houston, Texas.

Participating municipalities include Houston, Bellaire, Humble, Katy, and Hilshire Village.

Corpus Christi Crime Control and Prevention District
Purpose: Crime reduction/control program that may purchase police weapons and tools to be used in the field.

Participating municipality: Corpus Christi, Texas.

Scientific and Cultural Facilities District of Colorado
Purpose: Support art, culture, and scientific organizations in the Denver metropolitan area.

Participating municipalities include Adams, Arapahoe, Boulder, Broomfield, Denver, and Jefferson.

Los Angeles County Sales Tax for Homeless Services and Prevention
Purpose: Fund homelessness-related services and prevent homelessness.

Participating county: Los Angeles.

Miller Park Stadium Tax
Purpose: Finance and construct Miller Park stadium in Wisconsin.

Participating counties include Racine, Milwaukee, Waukesha, Washington, and Ozaukee.

When it comes to enacting tax laws, each tax entity will work independently of other tax entities and will work on its own schedule to design and implement tax laws and regulations or make changes thereto. Each tax entity will also define its own tax rates and will specify the dates when the tax rates become effective and expire.

The persons who authorize to enact tax laws and regulations and enforce them are the voters or elected officials. Voters will vote on propositions that involve the authorization of taxes and/or bonds that may lead to taxes. Elected officials will vote to enact new tax laws or make changes to existing laws. And the court systems will rule on cases that affect laws and policies and will issue mandates that may deem the tax laws enforceable or unenforceable.

After a change to a tax law is implemented, the tax entity will review its impact on the population and the economy. If the tax law is found to be very unpopular or is not producing the intended benefits, either more changes will be made to modify the law or the law may be voided, although it may take multiples changes before the laws and regulations are deemed to be producing their intended benefits. For other tax laws, no changes may be needed.

As changes are implemented by one tax entity, other tax entities will review these changes and consider their effect on the population, economies, and budgets. If the changes are considered beneficial and are achieving their intended purpose, the same process will be used to implement new tax laws or to modify the ones that are in place according to their jurisdictional reach. With this in mind, taxpayers can expect to see periodic changes to tax laws and regulations that follow the tax changes made by other tax entities.

RECIPROCAL TAX AGREEMENTS

Some tax entities will expand upon the benefits of their tax laws by participating in reciprocal tax agreements, which are established between two or more tax jurisdictions of the same tier with multiple goals in mind. In general, these agreements are intended to encourage the uniformity of tax rules and definitions, to level competition, and to enable retailers to collect taxes on remote sales for the participating entities.

Reciprocal tax agreements may affect any of your tax responsibilities that may be associated with interjurisdictional transactions. This may affect applicable taxes, tax rates, and any collection and/or remittance requirements. It may also affect the recognition of tax exemptions on taxable transactions and/or the exemption form that may be used when taking advantage of available exemptions.

Consideration: See Chapter 4: Tax Exemptions and Certifications for more information about taking advantage of applicable exemptions.

Some reciprocal agreements that have already been enacted for trade include the following:

US Interstate	Streamlined Sales and Use Tax Agreement (SSUTA)
	Multistate Tax Compact
International	Reciprocal Tariff Act of 1934
	Free Trade Agreements of the Americas (FTAA)
	North American Free Trade Agreement (NAFTA)

INFORMATION SHARING WITH TAXPAYERS

Tax authorities will deem taxpayers responsible for keeping up with the changes to tax laws. As changes to tax rates, laws, and regulations occur on different timelines, this can be challenging, time-consuming, and costly for the taxpayer. However, most tax entities are cognizant that taxpayers do encounter these challenges. They also recognize that it is beneficial to keep the taxpayer informed. Because of this, tax entities look for ways to make this process easier for taxpayers.

Tax entities use different tools for the sharing of tax information, such as mailing informational letters and brochures. Some tax entities will send tax information and updates via email if one provides them with one's email address. Websites are also made available whereon tax information is maintained for one to view. Helplines are also available for anyone to call and talk with someone qualified regarding the transactional taxes.

Seminars, another format used for the sharing of tax information and updates with taxpayers, are offered in some cities on an occasional or periodic basis. Tax authorities usually provide these seminars at no cost. Private business entities such as tax consulting firms also periodically offer seminars on taxes, some of which are customized for the customers' purpose. Keep in mind, though, that you might have to pay a fee to attend some of these seminars. Depending upon the provider and the platform of the presentation, you may have to travel to a designated location and be dependent on the schedule of the service provider. Presently, there is a growing trend of providing seminars using the internet.

With or without these tools, it is basically your responsibility to keep up with the changes to tax laws, regulations, rates, etc. You are also on your own when it comes to understanding how these things affect your activities. So, take advantage of the aforementioned tools as needed.

Emphasis: Along with taking advantage of these tools, do not hesitate to consult tax professionals and/or lawyers when needed.

TAX RESPONSIBILITIES RELATED TO TRANSACTIONS

For each transaction, there are generally two participants directly involved, and others involved indirectly. Each participant will have different responsibilities associated with the applicable transactional taxes. But all participants will have one responsibility in common, which is to be compliant with the tax responsibilities imposed upon each one of them.

Overall, the participants in transactional taxes include the following:

- tax authorities
- sellers
- buyers
- barterers
- businesses
- tax auditees
- tax professionals.

Following are general descriptions of some of the tax responsibilities that each of the different participants will be expected to address. These responsibilities and activities will be further elaborated upon in the following chapters.

Tax authorities or governments have the responsibility of defining, imposing, and enforcing tax laws and regulations. The tax laws and regulations will describe the object(s) of the transactional taxes, regulations, and policies. Tax authorities or governments also have the responsibility of defining how transactional taxes are to be collected and used. They will also describe how the collection and management of taxes may be completed and who is authorized to collect and manage them.

Tax authorities are also responsible for describing how they will enforce the tax laws and acquiring the tools they may use to do so. These tools are to be used to find incidents of noncompliance and to impose penalties. Some of the tools for tax audits include the use of mediation and courts. Of course, tax authorities will also describe the rights one has should one disagree with their findings and how to contest these findings.

Sellers have several responsibilities, including, when applicable, collecting tax exemption certificates (in lieu of collecting applicable transactional taxes) from their customers. Sellers also have to report and remit the collected taxes to the appropriate taxing entity or entities.

The seller's responsibilities require him or her to sufficiently understand each transaction and to identify whether he or she must bill any applicable transactional taxes for each of his or her transactions. For this, the seller must identify applicable tax, jurisdictions, and rates, and bill his or her customers for the applicable tax amounts. After collecting such taxes from the customer, the seller must report and remit the accrued taxes to the appropriate taxing entity using the appropriate forms and formats, such as using those found on the tax entity's website.

And, when given notice, sellers will have to address any inquiries by tax authorities and respond to any audits.

A **buyer**'s responsibilities include paying any transactional taxes that are imposed upon his or her procurement-related transactions or declaring a tax exemption by submitting the appropriate exemption certification form and/or documents for the taxable transaction.

If the buyer cannot take advantage of an exemption, he or she should ensure that the seller bills him or her for the applicable sales taxes.

When a seller does not bill the appropriate sales tax amount, the buyer should either request the seller to make the correction on his or her invoice or move to process the applicable use taxes and remit them to the appropriate taxing authority.

And, when given notice, buyers will have to address any inquiries by tax authorities and respond to any audits.

Barterers have a compound tax responsibility. As bartering involves buyers and sellers who trade goods, services, and/or monies in exchange for others' goods, services, and/or monies, it's possible that no currency will be exchanged, and instead a valuable will be exchanged. Tax entities view this type of transaction as one where the buyer is considered both a buyer and a seller and the seller is considered both a buyer and seller, and each of them bears the responsibility for any taxes imposed on their parts of the transaction.

Businesses as a whole also have a combination of tax responsibilities imposed upon them because their activities include both procurement (buying) and selling activities. Businesses also have tax-related reporting responsibilities.

Some businesses are required to register and acquire a **sales** tax permit, relevant license(s), and so forth when they develop a nexus in certain jurisdictions. These requirements are dependent upon the business's activities and upon requirements that have been defined by the relevant jurisdiction(s).

All businesses are required to remit all the taxes collected from their customers, pay use taxes, and complete tax returns as dictated by tax laws.

A **tax auditee** is one who has been selected by a tax authority to be audited. Such a person must cooperate with all tax auditors. When requested, the auditee must provide information and records to the auditors. To improve logistics, he or she may be asked to provide the auditors with a place to work on-site.

Auditees must pay any tax assessments resulting from tax audits. If the tax auditee disagrees with any tax assessment, then he or she has the right, which he or she should exercise, to contest the assessment if it is reasonable for the business to do so.

Tax professionals assist taxpayers in a variety of ways, such as answering specific tax questions, providing tax advice, managing tax audits, designing and/or implementing internal tax processes, and preparing tax returns.

A tax professional may be a direct employee of the taxpayer; a direct employee of a consulting or accounting firm who is hired to assist the taxpayer or his or her business; or a consultant or tax lawyer who is hired by the taxpayer. In general, a tax professional should be someone who is knowledgeable and has sufficient qualifications, certifications, and/or licenses to assist the taxpayer as the tax expert he or she represents himself or herself to be.

AGENTS OF TAX ENTITIES

Tax laws define either the buyer or seller in any transaction as an agent of the tax entity who will be deemed responsible for the billing, collecting, and/or remittance of applicable transactional taxes calculated on the transactions. The laws also describe the responsibilities and activities associated with the role of agent and the consequences for not complying with the responsibilities imposed upon the agents.

Most tax authorities will identify the seller as the agent who is responsible for the collection of the applicable taxes imposed upon transactions. However, some identify the buyer as the party responsible for the tax imposed on transactions and as their agent.

Regardless of whoever is defined as the agent, that individual must comply with his or her tax collection and remittance responsibilities. Each agent must remit the accrued taxes in a timely manner as defined by tax law and must use the appropriate tax forms or formats to remit these accrued monies, also indicating their source.

At no time should an agent keep any of the tax monies he or she has collected. If the collected tax and amount is appropriate, it must be remitted to the appropriate tax authority in a timely manner. If this unremitted money was billed and/or collected in error, then it should be returned to the customer in a timely manner. The consequences for not remitting the accrued monies in a timely manner include penalties, interest, and possibly criminal charges.

Each agent is expected to have the appropriate accounting processes, tools, and systems in place to enable him or her to comply with his or her tax responsibilities. Along with this, the tax authorities require the agent to keep records of the activities associated with the billing, collection, and remittance of sales, use, and any other transactional taxes. These expectations are further elaborated upon in the following chapters.

TAX REPORTING AND REMITTANCE

All taxpayers must comply with their tax reporting and remittance responsibilities in a timely manner. Following is a brief description of three key components for tax reporting and remittance. See chapter 6 for more details.

Tax reporting requires the completion and submittal of the appropriate tax returns provided by the relevant taxing authority.

Some tax authorities provide taxpayers with the ability to submit their returns online. Some tax authorities have made it a requirement that taxpayers complete their returns online. This trend of using online reporting tools is becoming more popular with tax authorities. So, check your tax authority's website to see if it has been designed with this capability and/or whether you are required to use it.

Tax remittance amounts that are due for any particular tax period are usually determined upon the completion of the tax return. Some tax authorities will allow a discount or credit to compensate the taxpayer for the collection and remittance of accrued sales taxes. Still, any amount owed must be paid in a timely manner, or else interest, late filing fees, and/or other penalties may be imposed.

If, after the completion of a tax return, you find that the amount owed is such that you are unable to make a lump-sum payment, contact your tax authority and ask for authorization to follow a payment plan. Some taxpayers are allowed to set up their own payment plans. However, keep in mind that if your payment plan is approved, you must do your best to pay as agreed, or otherwise it might become more costly than you are able to afford.

Tax refunds or credits may also be determined upon the completion of a tax return. If you find that a refund or credit is due to you, it will more likely be applied to any balance owed before a check is issued.

Emphasis: Be sure to complete tax returns and submit them in a timely manner, as well as pay any balances. Otherwise, you will likely incur additional costs for the delay or avoidance of the payments.

TAX REPORTING PERIODS AND FREQUENCY

Taxpayers are required to complete their tax returns and perform other reporting responsibilities according to the time schedule set by tax authorities. A tax reporting period is a period of time used to determine tax liability. The first period for a business usually starts when the business's activities start, and the last period will end when the company's business activities end, that is, when the business is formed and when it is closed, respectively. However, in between the start-up and closing dates, the periods are usually based upon the volume and/or type of business activity.

Common tax periods include annual, semiannual, quarterly, and monthly. Some tax laws may include bimonthly and/or weekly tax periods. The length of a reporting period may be extended when the business's revenue decreases and may be shortened when its revenue increases. Basically, there is an inverse relationship between changes in the length of a reporting period and the business's revenue and tax remittance amounts.

The due dates for each of the reporting periods are usually twenty to thirty days after the closing of a reporting period. The due date may change according to certain situations, such as when the due date falls on a holiday. In this case, the due date will likely be extended to the next business day. Another situation is when a disaster is declared in the jurisdiction. Such a declaration usually allows the taxpayers more time to comply with their reporting requirements. For these exceptional situations, check with your tax authority to verify whether you are entitled to any extensions.

In general, tax authorities provide taxpayers with a schedule of the due dates for reporting when the taxpayer first registers his or her business. If the tax authority does not provide such information at that time, the

13

taxpayer may look on the tax authority's website for this information. Another option is that taxpayers may call or send an email to the taxing authority for information on the scheduled due dates.

TAX AUDITS

Another component of transactional taxes is the management of tax audits, which are used primarily to check a taxpayer's compliance with his or her tax responsibilities. An audit is also used to identify and collect any taxes due, along with associated fines, penalties, and/or interest. If any overpayments are identified, these will likely be refunded or applied to taxes owed. Tax auditors will also provide the auditee with a report describing areas of noncompliance and may also briefly explain weaknesses of his or her processes and procedures.

Not all taxpayers are audited on a regular basis, if they are audited at all. But if you are audited, you must cooperate with the auditor and must provide the relevant information and documentation as requested. This will include information regarding the organization, the owner(s), responsible personnel, and transactions. The scope and volume of information and documentation requested will vary with the type and scope of the audit being performed.

The auditor will conduct a review and analysis of the information and documentation that has been provided and will also use other information available to him or her from other resources to verify the auditee's data and/or help with the auditor's analysis. Using these items will help the auditor to achieve the end goal of the audit, which is to identify noncompliance, to calculate and collect any assessed taxes, and/or refund any overpayments.

After the auditor completes the audit, the auditee will be informed of his or her findings. If the auditee has excellent tax policies and practices in place, then he or she doesn't have much to worry about. However, if the auditee does not have excellent tax policies and practices, he or she will likely have to pay an assessment, penalties, and/or interest. Hopefully, the auditee will move to use the audit as a chance to strengthen any weaknesses that have been identified in his or her policies and procedures.

SUMMARY

Every society imposes taxes in order to finance it activities and services. It is the responsibility of the members of that society to comply with the tax laws.

The ultimate tax goal of every person and business should be to constantly strive to comply with all his, her, or its tax responsibilities and, at the same time, minimize tax costs. Understanding the components of taxation will definitely assist you in staying in compliant with your tax responsibilities. Above all, do not avoid paying taxes due, as it is illegal and can end up being costly.

Chapter 2

Tax Jurisdictions, Authorities, and Laws

This chapter is not intended to be a comprehensive course on lawmaking or government structures. Instead, it is intended to provide you with an overview of government entities and their lawmaking capabilities and to emphasize how laws will affect you and your taxes. This chapter primarily focuses on the laws enacted by tax authorities within the United States as these are most likely to affect your transactions.

Having a basic understanding of tax structures and processes will provide you with the knowledge to facilitate your inquiries, efficiently perform your research, and stay compliant with tax rules and regulations. It may also help you to finds ways to minimize your tax liability.

GOVERNMENT TIERS AND NOMENCLATURE

Every nation in this world establishes its own structure of government and its own laws. Along with this, each nation defines its government's upper tiers and the lower tiers. In the United States of America, the most common tiers are federal, state, county, and city.

The United States consists of several tiers of tax jurisdictions that generally coincide with the government's upper tiers and lower tiers. Most of the higher tiers have several lower tiers, which themselves have lower tiers. Almost all are designated as tax jurisdictions that are empowered to enact transactional tax laws.

Caveat: Most people think that the United States of America is made up of only fifty states. These people either have forgotten or never learned about the geographical territories and possessions, along with their lower tiers, that are also part of the United States.

The first jurisdictional tier of the United States is known as the federal or national level. The second tier consists of forty-six states, four commonwealths, one federal district (District of Columbia [a.k.a. Washington, DC]), six territories or insular areas, and a number of Indian (i.e., Native American) tribal organizations. The third tiers are known as counties, parishes, boroughs, special districts, municipalities, state-recognized tribes, and special districts. The fourth tiers are known as cities, towns, districts, corporations, and/or boroughs.

Table 2.1 lists most of the nomenclatures used by the different government tiers within the United States.

Tiers (subdivisions) of the government of the United States of America			
Top tier	Second tier	Third tier	Fourth tier
• federal • national • republic	• state • commonwealth • territory or insular area • special district • Indian (i.e., Native American) tribal organization	• county • parish • borough • municipality • state recognized tribe • special district	• authority • barrio • borough • chapter • city • district • municipal corporation • quasi-municipal corporation • town • township • unincorporated area • village or hamlet • other political subdivision

TABLE 2.1. Tiers of the government of the United States of America.

If you are wondering why there are so many different names for the different government tiers, then you will have to refer to the history of this nation and of the different regions. For the most part, the original method of organizing the region or territory strongly affected the naming of its lower tiers. An example of this is Louisiana, which uses *parish* to label its third tier, as opposed to using *county*. Louisiana was ruled by France and Spain before it became part of the United States. Both nations were officially Roman Catholic–influenced governments and used the names of ecclesiastical divisions as the names of their lower tiers. This naming structure was not changed when Louisiana became part of the United States.

From the tax perspective, it is important to be cognizant of the names of the different government tiers and their subdivisions, as this may be important when you need to do some research into taxes. For example, if you decide to research taxes for a particular state, let's say Texas, on the internet, you may not get the results you seek if you use the nomenclature employed by a state such as Pennsylvania. Texas uses *county* and *city*, whereas Pennsylvania also uses *borough* and *township*. The tax laws will make use of the terminology used to separate the state's jurisdictions. If you try to use the words related to Pennsylvania's lowers tiers when you are researching Texas's tax laws, you may not receive the results you expected. So, forgetting about this difference may cause your research to be ineffective.

LEVYING OF TAXES

Before an established government tier or tax entity may impose transactional taxes, it must be authorized by the constitution and/or the second government tier. After the tax entity is given this taxing authority, it becomes known as a taxing authority or taxing entity. Each of these taxing entities may differ from others in terms of economy, demographics, and social culture. These differences will lead to differences in tax laws, tax rates, and methods of enforcing tax law.

A common goal among all these taxing entities is to collect revenue in order to finance their government's budget and perform its governmental responsibilities. This is a constant reality that is one of the driving forces of tax audits.

As different government tiers, including the lower tiers, acquire the authority to impose taxes, the likely result is a combination of taxing entities taxing the same location. Some areas may be taxed only by the second-tier, or state-level, government. Some areas may be taxed by the state and the third tier, or county-level tier. Some areas may be taxed by the third tier as well as by multiple lower-level tiers. Because of overlapping jurisdictions, it is imperative that you be aware of the multiple government entities that have taxing authority over your transactions in specific locations.

STATUTES, LAWS, RULES, REGULATIONS, AND MORE

Because tax entities are diverse, there is also diversity in tax laws, tax rulings, and policies. In the United States, tax-related laws may be initiated and/or enforced by statutes, rules, regulations, court orders, tax policies, case rulings, and opinions. Of course, each of these must be initiated by the relevant government agency if it is to be enforceable within the relevant jurisdiction(s). But also be aware that some of these components may override other laws, rulings, and policies.

Prior to becoming a law, a tax bill is introduced into the legislative branch of government. Bills are written by legislative committees, who develop the bill, review it, and/or modify it in order to present it to the main legislative body for voting. Most bills will be modified to accommodate the interests of various parties. For this, legislators will consider input from committees that may have done some research and brainstorming for the bill. Others will accept input from their constituents, lobbyists, and protestors. When the bill is agreed upon and approved, it will be enacted into law.

All laws are enacted with an effective date, and most are likely to be enacted without an expiration date. However, some laws may be set with a deactivation or sunset date, or may eventually be voided.

There are different ways by which a law, or a part thereof, may be voided or modified. Sometimes, corrections or supplemental laws are enacted in order to correct or clarify the intent of the original law. Other times, an authority such as the court systems will issue rulings that affect the law's validity and interpretation.

All these laws, rulings, and so forth may be found using different resources. The easiest and most commonly used resources are those offered by tax entities via their websites and publications, which are usually free to access. One may also turn to information-sharing resources such as *Wikipedia*, tax lawyers, tax accounting firms, schools, and seminars. But before you depend upon any of these resources, be sure to check whether or not the information provided may indeed be relied upon.

Emphasis: Keep in mind that it is you, the taxpayer, who has the ultimate responsibility for keeping up with changes to the tax law and their impact on your activities.

Consideration: Some tax entities offer automatic notification of tax updates and/or publications. If so, consider adding your name to the distribution list. These resources are usually provided at no cost and may be sent via email.

VALIDITY OF TAX LAWS

Sometimes after tax laws are implemented, they may be found to be invalid or unenforceable, or it may be determined that they impose an undue burden upon taxpayers. When this occurs, the tax laws may be contested or questioned. The options available for contesting such laws within the legal system include petitioning tax appeal boards or the civil court. There are basically two paths for challenging a tax law: (1) the legislative process and (2) lawsuits and civil court.

Using lawsuits and a civil court, a petitioner may find that his or her case starts and ends at the local court level or that it may proceed through the court system all the way up to the United States Supreme Court. The resulting rulings may either reinforce the law in place or cause all or part of it to be declared unenforceable. But to pursue this option involves costs for legal representation and time.

Using the legislative process to contest a law involves introducing a bill to the legislative branch of government and moving it through the legislative process, which involves explaining the issue and convincing legislators to change the law. Some people use lobbyists for this purpose. Others do the lobbying work themselves. Regardless which method is used, this is a time-consuming exercise and will take some money, time, and effort to pursue.

The information on each law that is contested is recorded and made available to the public for review. Depending on the outcome, the contested tax law may be modified or voided—or it may be reinforced. Regardless of the results, the record will be made available for learning purposes or for the enforcement of the law in future cases.

COOPERATING TAX ENTITIES

Some tax entities have determined that it is beneficial to cooperate with other tax entities for the purpose of applying and enforcing transactional taxes and determining how to treat them. For this, they enter into reciprocal tax agreements. The goals of these types of agreements are multifold. They ensure equality in terms of taxes and the collection of the taxes. They enable a fairer balance of competitive trade advantage resulting from lower tax rates in one jurisdiction as compared to another, and they recognize exemptions. The cooperative agreement also results in the sharing of information such as noncompliant activities and parties, although the impact of these agreements will only involve and affect the jurisdictions of the participating tax entities.

Generally, the participants of a reciprocal tax agreement will be tax authorities or governments of the same tier. That is, states will participate in such agreements with other states, and nations will participate in such agreements with other nations. But be aware, not all states or nations participate in reciprocal agreements.

Before any such cooperative effort may start, the participating tax authorities will have to design an enforceable reciprocal tax agreement. Then laws will need to be enacted to authorize cooperation between the participating tax entities.

These tax agreements are similar to general tax laws in that they may be modified or deactivated in order to enhance their benefits and/ or enhance clarification and/or enforcement. Such agreements may stipulate a limited duration. They may also be invalidated. In general, if your transactions are affected by a reciprocal tax agreement, be aware of any changes made to it that may affect you.

UNDERSTANDING TAX LAWS

If you do not understand a tax law, be assured that several resources are available that you may use to gain some clarity on the tax law and its impact on you. Resources include (1) you (i.e., self-study), (2) tax expert(s), and (3) the staff of the tax authority. Any one of these options alone may be beneficial, or you may choose to use a combination of them. The most important point here is that you should use such resources when needed to ensure you are comfortable with your understanding of the tax laws.

Self-Study

Self-study is where you take time out to do your own research. You can access the tax laws, rulings, and so forth, do searches on the internet, and ask others for information. Your research activities may also include attending classes and/or seminars, reading books, or discussing your concerns with others.

Benefits include the following:

- You will become more exposed to the tax laws and increase your knowledge base and understanding.
- You will be able to make more informed decisions regarding tax issues.
- You will be better informed for future decisions and analyses.

Downsides include the following:

- This will likely cost you time and money.
- You may fail to interpret the tax law appropriately.
- You may review information that is not applicable to your situation.

Tax Experts

Tax experts, available as a resource, are people who are experienced and trained in taxes. They include tax lawyers, tax accountants, and those with sufficient experience and education in taxes or who have earned a tax certification. Look for tax experts who have the training, experience, and/or certification to provide you with tax-related services and/or advice pertaining to your issue.

Benefits include the following:

1) You will have assurance that someone who is familiar and experienced with tax law will assist you in understanding the tax laws, answer your tax questions, or clarify your tax issues.

2) The advice a tax expert gives you may be backed by a warranty or assurance that he or she will reimburse you if you incur a cost because of having acted on his or her advice.

3) It may be more efficient to rely on a tax expert as opposed to trying to do part or all of the research yourself. The tax expert should be very familiar with the tax issue or question and be readily able to respond to your inquiry. If not, the person should be much more efficient in doing any necessary research than you are.

4) These tax experts may give classes or seminars to share relevant information or to teach others.

Downsides include the following:

1) Tax experts likely charge a fee that may be considered too expensive.

2) They may misinterpret the facts and give you nonapplicable information or advice.

3) You may fail to provide all the relevant facts to the tax expert, and, in return, he or she may provide you with incorrect or inapplicable information or advice.

Tax Entity Staff

Most tax entities have staff available to address inquiries via the telephone, fax, and email, similar to a helpline.

Benefits include the following:

- You may receive some explanation of the applicability of the tax law from the tax entity's staff.
- You may receive some information and/or guidance regarding tax law.
- If the information received from a tax entity's staff is documented, you may use this as proof to support your position.
- The information provided may help you to refine and/or shorten your research activities.

Downsides include the following:

- The tax entity's staff may be just as inexperienced or less experienced than you and/or provide the wrong information for your situation.
- You may have to speak to multiple people to find the one who is sufficiently knowledgeable with regard to the subject matter and related facts.
- If you make the inquiry via telephone, you will not have documented proof of the information provided to you.

SUMMARY

Tax laws are enacted by different authorized tax authorities in order to provide revenue for the relevant jurisdiction(s). Items will be taxed or untaxed depending upon the economic status and needs of the jurisdiction(s). These needs will also be a factor in providing tax exemptions from taxes and determining those that may be allowed for certain business and industries.

It is imperative that you adhere to tax laws and government tax agreements and that you know how these impact your activities. It is the taxpayer's responsibility to be informed of any tax laws that are applicable to his or her transactions. Keeping informed of the latest changes is also the taxpayer's responsibility.

Use the resources that are available to you to learn about the latest changes and to consider changes to improve your tax procedures and/or policies. But be wary of the information provided by platforms such as publications, websites, and seminars, as these may share outdated information and/or misinformation.

Chapter 3

Tax Types

As you likely know, taxes are imposed on many different items and are determined by the value of these items. For the most part, taxes are calculated based on the value of income, property, transactions, and the transference of property and assets. The differences between taxes and the determination of when they are applicable depends upon the essence of the items being taxed. Basically, in order to identify which tax is applicable to your activity, you will need to understand the essence of the different taxes and their intended objects (targets).

I like to group taxes into four basic classifications. Doing so usually makes it easier to identify which taxes are transactional and which are not. These groupings are as follows:

- income
- ownership
- transactional
- transference.

See table 3.1 for a list of taxes grouped by these four classifications.

The trick is to understand the essence of the intended object of the tax and its reach. For this, I have provided a brief description of each classification, as follows:

Income taxes are imposed upon the income or profit earned by individuals or businesses. For an individual, this tax is imposed upon the amount paid to the individual as earnings, such as his or her labor or personal services, that is, wages and salary. For a business, this tax is based on the revenue or profits the business earns.

26

Ownership taxes are taxes that are imposed upon assets owned by the taxpayer, such as inventory, equipment, and real estate. These taxes are usually reported periodically. The most commonly known ownership tax is property tax.

Transactional taxes are taxes that are imposed upon transactions involving a sale, a rental, a trade, or the use, storage, or consumption of an item. This tax is imposed at the time the transaction or action occurs.

Transference taxes are taxes that are imposed upon the transference of an item from one person or business to another person or business. Actually, whether a tax will be imposed depends upon the transfer of the property's title.

As stated before, *Basics about Sales, Use, and Other Transactional Taxes* predominantly concentrates on transactional taxes, so it may be helpful to use the following table when trying to rule out nontransactional taxes. This table groups some of the most popular tax types using the aforementioned tax groupings.

Major classifications of taxes[1]			
Income	Transactional	Ownership	Transference
• Contractor's tax[2] • Dividend • Excess profits • Franchise • Insurance gains • Interest • Medicare • Patents and licensing rights fees • Payroll • Social security • Unemployment • Windfall profits • Workers' compensation	• Consumption or use • Contractor's tax[2] • Environmental • Excise • Export/import services • Fees • Foods and meals • Fuel excise (gasoline, diesel, etc.) • Goods • Gross receipts • Leases • Licenses • Lodging • Luxury • Motorized vehicles • Rentals • Sales • Securities turnover • Services • Tolls • Value-added tax (VAT)	• Assets • Education • Hospital • Inventory • Personal property • Real property	• Gift • Estate • Inheritance • Nontangible assets • Charity

TABLE 3.1. Major classifications of taxes.

[1] This list is not inclusive of all tax types.

[2] This tax is listed under both income and transactional because some states identify this tax as a sales tax, whereas others identify it as a tax on income since it is imposed on the revenue earned from a contractor's contract.

As you can see, the list of transactional taxes is the longest of all four groups. One reason for this is that there are many more types of identifiable transactions than there are types of income, ownership, and transference. Another reason is that the tax authorities are creative in their imposing of taxes.

In general, transactional taxes are intended to be imposed upon the end consumer or end user of the commodities. Some of these taxes are imposed upon the business user. Meanwhile, others are levied for the personal use of the commodities. And some taxes are imposed for the right to conduct business.

If you do not see a specific tax listed in table 3.1, you should do your best to understand the essence of the tax you're searching for. Try to classify it into one of these groups. By doing this, you should be better able to determine whether it is indeed a transactional tax and how it may impact your transaction(s) or activities.

Consideration: If you are not sure of the essence of the tax, you may call the tax authority's helpline or check their website. But before you do so, read the next section.

ESSENCE OF TRANSACTIONS

In order to determine which transactional tax is imposed upon a certain transaction, you must first identify the essence of the transaction.

Know that some tax laws and tax entities offer definitions and guidance that may be used to facilitate the identification of the essence of your transaction and expand on the application of the tax. You may also find some of the rulings issued by courts, attorney general opinions, and private letter rulings helpful. Tax auditors' manuals are also helpful. Use these as needed. You should be able to find such items on the tax authority's website.

When transactions are complicated, you may have to use a combination of the aforementioned tools in order to gain some clarity on the essence of the transaction.

The essence of a transaction will likely fall into one of the following categories:

1. Charity purpose or gift	6. Rental or lease
2. Consumption or use	7. Retail sales
3. Construction	8. Service or installation
4. Governmental or civil	9. Storage, possession, and control
5. Manufacture or fabrication	10. Wholesale sales

If you are not sure what the essence of a certain transaction is, try asking yourself the following types of questions, which should help you to arrive at an understanding:

- "What am I procuring?"
- "What do I intend to do with the acquired item? How is it to be used?"
- "Who is to be the end user of the item?"
- "What happens to the item after I take possession or control of it?"
- "What happens to the item after I use it?"
- "If I plan to give away the procured item and expect no payment from the recipient, who is the recipient? Is it a charity, family, friend, or a business?"

Some examples of transaction essences, along with both personal and business examples, are as follows:

Charity purpose or gift

> Personal: A donation to a religion or other nonprofit organization; giving a car to a child or relative.
> Business: A donation to United Way or another nonprofit organization.

Consumption or use

Personal: You buy canned foods to feed your family.
Business: You buy staples from an office supply store in order to staple together sheets of paper.

Construction

Personal: Remodeling of a residential bathroom, or building a swimming pool or a home.
Business: Building of a fabrication shop, chemical plant, or shopping mall.

Governmental or civil

Business: Building a bridge for public use; building a dam for energy generation.

Manufacture or fabrication

Business: Products are mass-manufactured to be sold to wholesalers, retailers, or consumers.
Business: Custom products are fabricated using inventory or parts provided by the customer.

Rental or lease

Personal: Rental of automobiles or yard equipment, or lease of an apartment.
Business: Rental of cranes, tools, equipment, or lodging, or lease of an office building.

Retail sales

Personal: A grocery store sells canned goods to consumers.
Business: A store sells office supplies for business users.

Service or installation

> Personal: Appliance repair, lawn mowing, gardening services, the installation of an air-conditioning unit.
>
> Business: Repair of tools, equipment, or machinery; jobsite cleaning; installation of a refrigeration unit in a client's building.

Storage, possession, and control

> Personal: You buy fertilizer to store in your garage for future use on your lawn.
>
> Business: You buy inventory for future use to manufacture products.

Wholesale sales

> Business: The manufacturer sells its products in large quantities to its distributors, who in turn sell the products to their customers.

COMPLEX TRANSACTIONS

Understanding the essence of a transaction may become complicated when the transaction includes some items that may be taxable and other items that are nontaxable. Some items may be nontaxable when sold alone, but when sold in combination with taxable items, these same items may become taxable. The essence of the transaction and its complexity must be clarified in order to determine the taxability of the transaction and minimize tax costs.

Generally, a transaction may be considered either simple or compound. A simple transaction is one where all the items procured have one essence and either all are taxable or are all nontaxable. A compound transaction is one with two or more subessences, and these combined become the primary essence of the transaction.

Following are three examples of transactions that should help to clarify the foregoing ideas:

Simple transaction

When you go to the bookstore, buy a book, and take it home for recreational reading, the essence of this transaction is the purchase of the book for your personal use. Usually, this is a taxable purchase for the buyer.

Compound transaction

You buy a refrigerator from seller A, who is located in the same city as you. You also agree that seller A will deliver and install the refrigerator and that seller A will charge you for the associated delivery and installation service. Along with this, you are not able to declare an exemption from the imposed transactional taxes.

The essence of this transaction is the sale of the refrigerator for personal use. The delivery and installation service charges are secondary yet, at the same time, essential to the purchase. Basically, if the refrigerator is not purchased, there is no need to pay the delivery and installation charges.

Most tax authorities will consider that the selling price of the refrigerator is comprised of both parts of this transaction. In effect, the complete invoice price will be considered taxable. In other words, you are buying an item whose components (refrigerator, delivery, and installation) are considered as one purchase. However, you should check whether the applicable tax laws will consider the shipping and delivery charge to be nontaxable if separately listed from the delivered items.

For compound transactions, some tax entities use a "true object test" or an "essence rule" in order to identify the ultimate taxability of the transaction. One such rule is that if the transaction is composed of 95 percent taxable items, then the entire transaction is considered taxable. Look for rules such as these to be embedded in tax laws and policies.

Separated transactions

You buy a refrigerator from seller A. Afterward, you hire seller B to pick up the refrigerator, deliver it, and install it in your home.

This example involves two independent simple transactions that are required to complete the ultimate goal. The two simple transactions are as follows:

1) the purchase of the refrigerator from seller A and

2) the purchase of services (pickup, delivery, and installation) from seller B.

When considering the taxability of each transaction, you should view each as a transaction independent of the other. The refrigerator is usually taxable. The delivery and installation services are usually nontaxable.

When analyzing simple, compound, or separated transactions, you should consider several factors, including the following:

1) the ultimate essence or purpose of each transaction

2) the applicable tax rules associated with the use or disposition of the procured items.

Be Aware: The actual taxability of these transactions is based on the tax laws of the relevant taxing jurisdictions and the applicability of these laws to your particular situation.

COMMON TRANSACTIONAL TAXES

In this section, I mention some of the most common tax types and provide a brief description of each. This list is intended to serve as a basic introduction to each tax type so you may understand whether these may be applicable to your transaction. Keep in mind, however, that some taxing entities may use different names or labels for similar tax types.

Again, I provide only a brief description because the purpose of *Basics about Sales, Use, and Other Transactional Taxes* is to serve only as an introduction to the topics herein. If you feel this is an insufficient amount of information to help you understand the tax, then you should do some research and/or consult other resources to gather more details and/or clarification.

Contractor's Tax

This is a tax imposed on the gross receipts of the transactions made by a construction contractor. Usually, this tax is paid by the prime contractor; however, some states may impose this tax on subcontractors if the prime contractor fails to pay the tax.

Diesel or Kerosene Fuel

This is a fuel tax imposed upon diesel or kerosene used primarily for on-road purposes. Generally, this fuel is undyed so it may be identified as a taxable fuel. If diesel fuel or kerosene is intended to be sold for nontaxable purposes, it is dyed red to distinguish it from taxable fuels.

Dyed Diesel or Dyed Kerosene

This is a fuel tax imposed upon diesel or kerosene that has been dyed red. The purpose of the red dye is to identify the fuel as nontaxable and to specify that it is to be used with off-road equipment, such as for farm or construction purposes.

Most dyed fuels are used off-road and are either untaxed or minimally taxed.

This type of fuel is also known as marked fuel, red-dyed diesel, or farm fuel.

Environmental

This tax, imposed upon products that have been identified as somewhat
harmful to the environment, is intended to provide an incentive
to reduce certain emissions and to fund services that may benefit
the environment.

This tax is also known as ecotax, pollution tax, or green tax.

Excise

This tax is imposed upon two population groups: (1) sellers and/or
manufacturers of specific goods or (2) buyers of specific goods.
If it is imposed upon the seller, then this tax may be passed onto
or directly billed to the consumer of the goods as part of the
selling price.

This type of tax is usually imposed upon goods that are not
essential to survival, such as alcoholic beverages and cigarettes.

Usually, one will see a stamp placed upon the goods indicating
that the excise tax has been paid.

Export

This tax, imposed by customs authorities or a federal taxing authority,
is imposed upon goods when they are leaving one country for
export to another country.

This tax may also be known as transit duty, export duty, or
customs tax.

Fees

From a tax perspective, fees are usually taxes that are levied upon a
service.

Examples of fees include costs to enter a park or the cost to
dispose of a tire.

Note: Sometimes a tax may be labeled as a fee. When this occurs, there are usually political reasons behind it. Politicians do not like to utter the words "We need to levy a tax for ..." because taxpayers tend to react more negatively to the word *tax* than to the word *fee*.

Fuel

Fuel tax is an excise tax that is imposed on various motor fuels, such as gasoline, diesel, and gasohol. The tax is usually imposed upon the seller and may be passed onto the buyer as an indirect tax.

Several government tiers may levy this tax, including the federal tier, the state tier, and local tier.

This tax is also known as petrol tax, gasoline tax, gas tax, or fuel duty.

Goods and Services

This tax, levied upon the sales price of the goods and services that are procured, is usually imposed upon the buyer and is collected by the seller, who in turn remits it to the appropriate taxing authority.

Gross Receipts

This is similar to a sales tax, although instead of being levied upon the buyer, it is levied upon the seller of goods and/or services. This tax is based upon the total gross receipts of the transaction.

In some jurisdictions, this tax may also be known as a gross excise tax.

Heavy Equipment

This is a tax that has some variations and is levied upon the gross receipts derived from the sale, lease, or short-term rental of heavy equipment. Some tax authorities impose this tax upon heavy equipment dealers that offer the rent or lease of the equipment at retail for short terms. This tax may be recovered as a pass-through tax from the rentee or leasee. Others impose this tax on the rentee or buyer of heavy equipment. Overall, this tax is not a sales or use tax and should be billed as a separate line item from other taxes and costs billed.

Tax authorities generally define heavy equipment as being mobile, used for construction and industrial applications, and being without an operator. Other descriptors include a minimum weight and fuel type.

Usually, this tax is a substitution for a property tax, and its recovery is assessed upon short-term rentals or leases of heavy equipment.

This is also known as special inventory tax, HET, or unit property tax.

Import

Import tax is imposed by customs authorities upon goods as they are entering one country as an import from another country.

Depending on the goods to be imported, this may also be known as a customs duty or tariff.

Lease

Lease tax, similar to rental tax and sales tax, is levied upon the price (sale) of the item leased.

Most tax entities consider leases to involve a period of more than twenty-eight or thirty days.

License

A license fee is basically a tax paid to a government for the privilege of conducting an activity, such as operating a business, practicing a vocation, hunting, or driving a car.

Some licenses may be issued for a limited period of time and may be renewed as long as the fees are paid and the associated requirements have been met. Other licenses may be perpetual in duration.

Luxury

This tax is levied upon items that are considered nonessential or unnecessary, such as luxury goods, which include expensive cars, jewelry, yachts, and private jets.

Registration Fee

This tax is imposed when the title of a specific asset is transferred from the seller to the buyer or when the item is gifted by a donor to a recipient.

The assets may include automobiles, trailers, or property deeds.

This tax may also be known as a title transfer fee.

Rent

This is similar to sales tax or lease tax. It is levied upon the rental price (sale) of the item rented. It should be collected by the renter from the rentee or tenant and, in turn, be remitted to the applicable taxing authority.

Most tax entities consider a rental period to be less than twenty-eight or thirty days. If it the rental period exceeds the defined limit, it will be considered a lease.

Sales

This is a tax levied upon the sale of certain goods and services. It is imposed upon the buyer and is collected by the seller, who in turn remits it to the applicable taxing authority.

Usually, sales taxes are not imposed upon items essential for survival, such as foods, pharmaceuticals, and medical services.

Surcharge

This is an additional cost or tax levied upon specific goods or services. It is a separate charge from the standard transactional taxes. When imposed, the surcharged is billed to the buyer and should be listed separately from any other transactional taxes.

The surcharge may also be known as surtax.

Example: Some telecommunications companies bill surcharges to recover their federal Universal Service charge, regulatory charges, and other such related costs. You will see these listed separately on the bill issued to you.

Note: Some surcharges may be considered taxable.

Title Transfer Fee

Similar to a registration fee, a title transfer fee is levied upon the transference of an asset when this transference is registered with the appropriate tax authority.

Assets may include automobiles, trailers, and property deeds.

This fee may also be known as a registration fee.

Tolls

A toll is a tax levied for the privilege or liberty of doing something such as passing over a bridge or driving on a stretch of highway.

This is also considered to be a use tax.

Use

Use tax is levied upon the value of an item or a service by the tax jurisdiction where the item is located or the service is performed and when the item is used, stored, or consumed if sales taxes have not already been paid for such item.

Basically, use tax is complementary to sales taxes. If the applicable sales tax is not paid to a seller, then the buyer is likely required to pay applicable use taxes.

The use tax will be calculated based on the cost of the item used or service consumed and will be remitted directly to the applicable taxing authority.

Value-Added Tax (VAT)

This is a tax levied upon a good and service when value is added to it at each stage of its production or development and at its final sale. This is also considered a consumption tax.

At this time, this tax type is not levied in the United States. Instead, it is more common in countries such as Canada and Trinidad and Tobago and in most European countries.

Vice Tax

This is an excise tax levied upon goods that have been deemed to be harmful to society. Examples include alcohol, cigarettes, soft drinks, and fast foods. Usually, vice tax is levied upon items procured for personal use.

This tax may also be known as a sin tax or sumptuary tax.

INDUSTRY-SPECIFIC TAXES

Most states have enacted industry-specific taxes, that is, taxes designed to affect specific industries. These are taxes that replace the standard sales/use taxes, with rates that are usually lower than the standard defined sales/use tax rates. The primary purpose of this type of tax is to invite and retain businesses that the tax authorities deem beneficial to its jurisdiction.

Businesses should keep in mind that the list of industries that are given these special tax rates may differ for each taxing jurisdiction. Also, these taxes are apt to change as the economic needs of the taxing jurisdiction changes.

Usually, changes are made to the laws governing these industry-specific taxes when the industry is deemed to be no longer economically beneficial to the jurisdiction, although some business entities may be able to lobby for special tax breaks based on their business volume and/or the positive impact they make on the jurisdiction.

Following is a list of industries and groups that may benefit from industry-specific taxes:

- Agriculture
- Computer sales and service
- Contractor
- Customs brokers
- Data centers
- Data processing
- Dude or guest ranch

- Lodging
- Mining
- Offshore exploration
- Oil and gas
- Photography
- Publishing

- Fuel refinery
- Research and development
- Restaurant
- Schools
- Taxidermy
- Telecommunications
- Timber

Note: Because these industries are given special treatment, some of the taxing jurisdictions require the business to apply for a special certification or permit that formally recognizes its business activities.

REIMBURSABLE PASS-THROUGH TAXES

Technically, all businesses pass their costs of doing business on to their buyers, including their tax costs. Some tax costs are embedded in the selling price, where the buyer does not see a separate line item for the seller's tax cost. However, some tax costs may have to be billed separately to the buyer so he or she may see and pay these costs so as to be reimbursed later. This type of tax is commonly known as a reimbursable pass-through tax and is considered part of the amount to be paid by the buyer.

Reimbursable pass-through taxes are usually associated with specific types of items, such as assets or heavy equipment. Or this tax may be associated with expenses that are reimbursable by the buyer based on a contractual agreement.

Should the seller decide to directly bill the buyer for the recovery of this cost, then the seller should list it as a separate line item on the buyer's invoice. The accompanying description should note that the cost is for the reimbursement of the seller's tax, for example, "reimbursement of heavy equipment tax," not something like "heavy equipment tax."

Depending on the tax, some buyers may benefit from the seller's practice of separately listing the reimbursable pass-through taxes. For some transactions, no markups may be imposed on the pass-through tax. That is, profit should not be sought in the billing for these taxes. For other transactions, the buyer may use the invoice to request a refund of the pass-through tax from the relevant tax authority if he or she has the authority to do so.

Following are conditions that a seller must meet in order to be able to bill the pass-through tax to his or her customer:

1) The seller has paid the tax to the relevant taxing authority.

2) The tax to be reimbursed must be described as the reimbursement of the pass-through tax on the buyer's invoice.

3) The tax must be listed as a separate line item on the buyer's invoice in a place where the buyer can identify it as such.

Adhering to these conditions will minimize confusion over what tax is being billed to the buyer. It will clearly identify a reimbursement tax, distinguishing it from the tax that has been imposed upon and billed to the buyer. Also, some tax entities require the separate listing of this pass-through tax before certain buyers (i.e., manufacturers) may request a refund of it.

Following are two examples of invoice layouts whose line items reflect the billing of reimbursement of pass-through taxes.

Example 1. This invoice layout reflects the billing of the end customer for the reimbursable taxes that the seller has paid previously.

RENTAL INVOICE

Seller:	Widget Rentals Inc. 111 Main St. City, State 11111	**Buyer:**	Equipment User Inc. 300 Main St. City, State 22222	**Invoice No.** Invoice date: Ship via: Rental start: Rental end:	AA-123 6/8/2022 Fast delivery 6/1/2022 6/7/2022
Remit:	Widget Rentals Inc. PO Box 123 City, State 11111-0123	**Ship-To:**	Equipment User Inc. 300 Main St. City, State 22222	FOB: Terms:	City, State Net 30 days

Line	Quantity	Item description	Unit cost	Line total	Tax
1	20	Widget rental	$100.00	$2,000.00	T
2	20	**Reimbursement of property tax on widget**	**$2.00**	**$40.00**	T
3	1	Shipping and delivery charges	$50.00	$50.00	T
4	1	10% markup (on items 1 and 3)	$209.00	$209.00	T
			Subtotal:	$2,299.00	
			Sales tax (8.25%):	$189.67	
			Invoice total:	$2,488.67	

Taxable amount= $2,299.00

Note: For this example, the buyer did not issue an exemption certificate to the seller.

Example 2. This invoice reflects the billing of expenses where the seller paid sales taxes on materials (pipe) to his vendor and where the end customer had agreed to pay a 10 percent markup on all costs associated with the items except the sales taxes paid. This usually occurs for a sale whose pricing agreement is based on billing for time and materials, such as in the construction industry.

SALES INVOICE

Seller:	Builder Inc. 111 Main St. City, State 11111	**Buyer:**	Refinery Inc. 300 Main St. City, State 22222	**Invoice no.**	AA-123
				Invoice date:	6/8/2022
				Ship via:	Fast delivery
				Rental start:	6/1/2022
Remit:	Builder Inc. PO Box 123 City, State 11111-0123	**Ship-To:**	Refinery Inc. 300 Main St. City, State 22222	Rental end:	6/7/2022
				FOB:	City, State
				Terms:	Net 30 days

Line	Quantity	Item description	Unit cost	Line total	Tax
1	20	Pipe	$100.00	$2,000.00	NT
2	1	**Reimbursement of sales taxes paid on pipe**	**$165.00**	**$165.00**	NT
3	10	Labor	50.00	500.00	NT
4	1	Shipping and handling charges	$25.00	$25.00	NT
5	1	10% markup (on lines 1, 3 and 4)	$252.50	$252.50	NT
			Subtotal:	$2,942.50	
			Sales tax[1] (8.25%):	$0.00	
			Invoice total:	$2,942.50	

Taxable amount = $0.00

Note: For this example, the buyer did not have to issue an exemption certificate to the seller as this sale is not taxable. The builder is considered the consumer of the material (pipe) and paid taxes on the pipe. The buyer is a refiner and will be able to request reimbursement of the sales taxes paid by the seller using this invoice.

45

TRANSACTIONAL TAXES IN TERRITORIES OF UNITED STATES

At this time, the United States has fourteen territories or possessions, five of which are considered inhabited and which do impose taxes. Their tax structures have some similarities to the tax structures of some of the mainland states, and as it is with any tax laws, these are subject to change.

The following is a list of the inhabited territories and brief information regarding the taxes imposed by each:

American Samoa

- Imposes a general import tax
- Does not impose a sales tax.

Guam

- Imposes a 2 percent sales tax that took effect on October 1, 2018.
- Local taxes on products such as liquor, tobacco, gasoline, real property, gross receipts, use, admissions, amusement, recreational facilities, and hotel occupancy.

Northern Mariana Islands

- No sales taxes imposed.
- Imposes a gross receipts tax.

Puerto Rico

- General sales tax imposed at the territorial tier.
- Some local sales tax.

US Virgin Islands

- No sales taxes.
- Imposes a gross receipts tax.
- Excise tax and customs duties.

As with any of the mainland taxes, look for exemptions from the sales tax and any limitations on its applicability. Another consideration is minimum thresholds before any taxes or fees are applied, such as gross receipt taxes, excise taxes, and/or customs duties. And, as with any tax, look for expiration dates, and/or any change to the tax rate. Also look for any new taxes.

INTERNATIONAL-RELATED TAXES

As you surely know, we live in a global economy where we may easily conduct business with sellers and buyers who are located in other nations. For international-based transactions, sellers and buyers should consider whether their tax liability may be extended to jurisdictions of the originating and/or destination nations. Businesses should identify and quantify how much of an impact the international taxes will make on its costs, prices, and responsibilities.

Depending on the participating nations of an international transaction, the traders may have to pay transactional taxes to the tax authority of the originating nation and to that of the destination nation. Traders may also have to pay duties and other costs associated with the importation and/or exportation of their goods. Sometimes, bonds are required to ensure payments. All these taxes, customs fees, and related charges must be paid unless there is a tax treaty in place whose benefits (e.g., exemptions) you can take advantage of to minimize your taxes and costs.

As you move to identify what taxes apply to your international transactions, you may have to research the tax laws of other relevant nations or depend upon licensed customs brokers or consultants to explain the requirements. Traders should research import/export laws and applicable tax costs for the goods imported or exported. International traders should become familiar with, and stay familiar with, active trade agreements and laws that may describe which taxes can or cannot be reduced or eliminated.

Some of the mechanisms that can help sellers and/or buyers to identify, understand, and minimize the taxes that may be imposed upon their international transactions include the following:

- **Trade agreements**, which describe the scope of taxes, exemptions, any exceptions, and durations.
- **Customs requirements** for importing and exporting goods that describe regulations, requirements for paying taxes and fees, packaging, shipping and delivery, proof of identification, and other related information.
- **Declaration and reporting forms** to import goods, including entry manifests, bonds, evidence of right to make entry, a commercial or pro forma invoice, and packing lists (if appropriate), among other necessary documents.

Note: Invoices are used to declare the value of the goods, which may be used to determine which taxes and fees are applicable.

Customs brokers will help the importer and/or exporter to meet the governmental requirements for the import and export activities and also provide other services.

Emphasis: When participating in international trade, be sure to properly complete the appropriate forms and provide the required documents. Failure to do so will surely cause delays in delivery and/or unnecessary costs.

SUMMARY

Just as surely as there are many different types of transactional taxes, there are likely to be modifications to the tax laws. New tax laws may be enacted. Present tax laws, rates, and rulings may be changed, replaced, or deactivated. With this in mind, each taxpayer should be cognizant that there is no regular schedule for modifying tax laws and rates. Instead, these are implemented when defined. The task of staying informed of these changes and knowing when they occur may not be easy, but it is necessary.

When considering the task of keeping informed, consider a strategy for managing the full scope of this task. As part of this strategy, consider the following:

1. Identify which taxes and tax laws are most relevant to your activity.

2. Identify and utilize the tools and resources that are most beneficial for your research / collection of information and any changes associated with it.

3. Determine when and how to promptly act on the changes that affect your business and/or personal transactions.

Chapter 4

Tax Exemptions and Certifications

Just as transactional tax laws are enacted or changed, exemptions related to those taxes are considered, made available to taxpayers, or canceled. Tax exemptions may allow the buyer or seller to be exempt from part of or all the transactional taxes imposed on a transaction. Or the scope of the exemption may be limited to some of the items, under specific conditions. Overall, these exemptions are intended to benefit the buyer and/or seller whose transaction(s) meet(s) the established criteria and to encourage business.

In order for a taxpayer to take advantage of an exemption, an exemption declaration must be made in a timely manner. The declaration will involve the presentation of the appropriate exemption forms and/or supporting documentation to the seller. The requirements, forms, and documentation will be described in more detail in the following sections. But keep in mind that one must save the exemption declarations and their supporting documents in case of an audit.

AUTHORIZATION OF TAX EXEMPTIONS

There are at least two groups of tax authorities that may empower taxpayers with the authority to declare an exemption from transactional taxes. The first group includes legislators who introduce exemptions via the legislative process. The second group includes those who have been granted the authority to grant exemptions by way of legislation. These include empowered authorities and boards.

Each tax authority will define and describe the following:

1) available tax exemptions,

2) criteria under which each exemption may be applicable, and

3) exemption forms and documentation required to be used and shared when a buyer is declaring the exemption.

This information may be found within the statutes of the relevant taxing authority and on websites and in publications supported by the tax authority.

It is important to know that tax exemptions will vary just as taxes vary. Some exemptions may be applied to the total amount of tax imposed upon a transaction or to a part thereof. Some may be in the form of a discount, credit, or rebate. Also, tax exemptions are made available to some industries, some activities, some goods, and/or some services. Some exemptions may be granted for only a limited period of time.

Consideration: Tax exemptions are not applicable to items that are not taxed. So, if your seller asks for an exemption certificate on a nontaxed item, take the time to explain that an exemption certificate is not technically applicable. Or use an exemption form where you may note that the items to be procured are not taxed by legislation.

RESPONSIBILITIES ASSOCIATED WITH TAX EXEMPTIONS

To take advantage of an exemption on transactional taxes, each party participating in the transaction must carry out their responsibilities as defined by the taxing authorities. They must also comply with any specific time lines for seeing to these responsibilities.

Two things that a taxpayer can depend upon is that tax authorities constantly strive to identify those who are in noncompliance with their tax responsibilities and to enforce their tax laws. If the taxpayer fails to meet his or her responsibilities, then he or she may have to pay more than just the originally imposed tax amount because of interest and penalties. Be assured that the tax authorities want all the tax monies owed to them.

51

However, there are exceptions allowed for some tax responsibilities. These are granted for exceptional situations, usually unforeseen events such as declared disasters. Most commonly, the time allowed for compliance will be extended instead of alleviating the responsibility. However, one must prove to the tax authority that one is entitled to such an exception as an excuse for not paying the taxes.

Following are some common responsibilities that buyers and sellers should strongly consider and adhere to when completing transactions:

Sellers

- Sellers must consider all transactions to be taxable unless the item to be sold has been designated as a nontaxed item or the buyer provides the appropriate exemption certificate to the seller in a timely manner.
- If the seller has been provided with an exemption certificate, then he or she is required to review it for validity. If it is found to be invalid or questionable, the seller must ask the buyer to provide an exemption certificate that is relevant and properly completed.
- If the seller has not received a valid exemption certificate from the buyer, the seller must bill any applicable tax to the buyer.
- The seller must keep all exemption certificates on file as long as is designated by the applicable taxing authority.
- If a tax auditor asks a seller for proof of exemption or other information, the seller should cooperate and provide such to the tax auditor as requested.

Buyers

- Buyers should review each of their transactions and to determine taxability.
- If a seller asks the buyer for an exemption certificate for a certain transaction, the the buyer should provide such when applicable.
- If a buyer intends to declare an exemption on a transaction, then he or she must inform the seller of this and provide the seller with the appropriate documentation declaring the exemption.

- If a buyer cannot declare an exemption, then he or she should ask the seller to bill the appropriate transactional taxes.
- Every exemption certificate should be properly completed and provided to the seller in a timely manner as required by law.
- When a seller does not include the applicable transactional tax on the invoice, the buyer must remit the appropriate use taxes (also called consumption taxes) to the appropriate tax authorities.
- When required, each business must register with the appropriate government agency or agencies before taking advantage of an exemption.

TAX EXEMPTION DECLARATION FORMS

A variety of exemption forms and/or documents have been designed for declaring an exemption. Each tax authority defines which forms, documents, and information is to be provided to the seller when declaring an exemption. Different jurisdictions may use differently laid out exemption forms and other documents, but at a minimum, this paperwork will provide similar information to the sellers.

The tax exemption form or document you will use depends on the type of exemption to be taken and by whom it is legally recognized. Some tax authorities require the use of different forms based on how the taxable items are to be consumed or disposed of, such as reselling the items versus using them to manufacture a product. Some forms are industry-specific such as those for manufacturers or refineries. Some are based on special taxing authorities, and some are based on tax agreements. Since there is a variety of exemption forms available, you should try to understand the basis of your exemption in order to select the appropriate form.

Another consideration is that the taxing authority may periodically modify the exemption certification forms. So, be sure to check for the latest forms and documentation requirements from time to time. The latest forms (including their requirements) may be found on the tax entity's website or office and/or from other authorized sources. Other resources include private tax software programs, tax professionals, and tax lawyers.

Some tax authorities allow some taxpayers to design their own tax exemption forms. This may facilitate the reading of the document and minimize confusion by eliminating unrelated text or emphasizing relevant data. However, these customized forms must adhere to the tax laws and include the information that these require. Some of these forms may need to be approved by the tax authorities before use.

Tip: When declaring an exemption from taxes, be sure to use the appropriate form and provide all the required documentation and information to the seller. And don't forget to sign!

EXEMPTIONS FROM THE SELLER'S PERSPECTIVE

When a tax authority deems a seller as its agent, the seller acquires certain responsibilities: billing the buyer for applicable transactional taxes or collecting and storing any exemption certification the buyer offers. If the buyer does not provide the appropriate exemption documentation, the seller must bill the buyer for the applicable transactional taxes and remit these to the appropriate tax authorities.

Technically, if a buyer does not present an exemption certificate to the seller when placing his or her order for taxable items, the seller should ask for it. However, sometimes a seller will request exemption certification from the buyer for one or more orders after the orders are completed. Other times, these requests are initiated as a result of an internal audit or an audit of the seller.

Use of blanket or semiblanket exemption certificates will provide some convenience for both the seller and buyer as then they will not have to generate and/or collect exemption certificates for each individual purchase order. However, the seller must be sure to keep this paperwork for each applicable order, ensure that it does not expire, and determine whether it is applicable to any new orders placed.

A blanket exemption certificate will become invalid when a seller receives a notice from the buyer regarding his or her intent to revoke the exemption certificate. It will also become invalid in situations where the buyer's sales tax permit or direct payment permit is no longer valid. To prevent any undesirable consequence(s) from an invalid blanket exemption certificate, sellers should periodically review the validity of each certificate.

Some semiblanket exemption certificates may have an expiration date. Sellers must not apply this exemption certificate to a sales order that has been placed after the expiration date has passed. Instead, the seller should make a request to the buyer for a replacement or should start billing applicable taxes.

The type of filing system a seller uses to store exemption documentation depends on the seller's recordkeeping style. Some sellers may file this paperwork alphabetically by buyer name and/or use an internal control number such as the buyer's account, purchase order, or invoice number. Some will attach the exemption documents to the original order or invoice. Regardless of the filing system used, it should be consistent and allow for the easy retrieval of the documents.

Sellers should also have a method to easily identify expiring, expired, and/or limited exemption certificates. This, in turn, should enable a seller to easily determine when it is time to ask for a replacement exemption certificate.

Emphasis: The seller must either collect an exemption certificate from the buyer for the purchase or must bill for applicable taxes on taxable items.

EXEMPTIONS FROM THE BUYER'S PERSPECTIVE

Most tax authorities hold buyers responsible for paying applicable transactional taxes or, in lieu of this, issue an exemption declaration associated with the taxable items. It is the buyer's responsibility to determine whether his or her purchase is taxable or not and, if so, whether he or she may declare an exemption. For this and other reasons, it would be smart for the buyer to be familiar with the exemptions available for his or her transactions and use them appropriately.

When a buyer issues a purchase order, he or she should review it in order to determine which exemption is applicable. The buyer should not rely on a seller to determine the tax status of his or her order. Sometimes a seller, not fully understanding the purpose of the order and/or the tax laws, may provide misleading advice to the buyer. Ultimately, the buyer will be held responsible for applicable taxes even if he or she followed the seller's guidance and suggestions.

If the buyer decides to take advantage of an exemption, he or she must provide the seller with the appropriate exemption certificate and/or documentation. If the seller bills the appropriate taxes, then the buyer should be sure that the seller is authorized to do so. If the order is not taxable, the buyer should be sure that the seller is aware of this. These steps will help to keep the buyer compliant with his or her tax responsibilities and avoid unnecessary costs and/or problems.

After a buyer issues an exemption certificate to the seller, he or she should keep a record or a copy of it. There are a few benefits for doing this. One is the ability to track details such as which transactions have an exemption certificate and by whom it was issued. Another is the ability to determine when to retract or deactivate an exemption declaration. A third is that this may demonstrate to internal and/or external auditors that the tax-related procedures have been established and are being adhered to.

Tip: The buyer is the one who must decide whether to take advantage of any exemption and, if so, the one who must provide the seller with the appropriate exemption certification form and/or documents if he or she so decides.

VALIDITY OF EXEMPTION CERTIFICATES

An exemption certificate is considered a legal document. Because of this, upon signing an exemption certificate, the buyer is swearing that, to the best of his or her knowledge, the information he or she is providing is accurate and true. If it is discovered that the buyer has provided inaccurate or false information, then consequences such as penalties, fines, and even jail time may be imposed upon the offender. Therefore, it is important that the documents completed for each exemption declaration be reviewed for compliance with the requirements of the taxing authorities.

Certain information must be provided on the forms. If you are not sure what information you'll need to complete the form(s), you should check for the instructions on the tax authority's website. Another option is to ask your favorite tax consultant for assistance.

Emphasis: An exemption certificate must be completed with the appropriate information and signed.

Following is a quick list of what to look for when reviewing an exemption certificate for validity. Make sure that the following information is provided:

- legal **names** of the buyer and seller
- **addresses** of the buyer and seller
- **identification number** of the taxpayer declaring the exemption

> *Note:* Some exemption certificates may not require this information. Others require that the buyer acquire a sales tax permit or register his or her business before being authorized to issue the exemption certificate.

- **reason or basis** for the declaration of the exemption
- **description** of what is being procured
- **signature** of an authorized representative of the buyer
- **date** when the form is signed.

SCOPE OF EXEMPTION CERTIFICATION

When a buyer issues an exemption certificate, he or she must define the scope of the exemption, which involves describing what is procured and to what extent the exemption applies. This will indicate that the exemption either applies to all transactions or is limited in scope.

Basically, there are three types of scopes used for exemption certificates. They are as follows:

1. blanket exemption

2. semiblanket or a limited exemption

3. specific exemption or very limited exemption.

With a **blanket exemption,** the buyer is declaring exemption from all transactional taxes applicable to all orders placed with the seller.

Sample descriptions are as follows:

o "All purchases made."
o "All tangible personal properties and taxable services procured."

Some forms, such as the direct payment exemption certificate, may not require a description. In such cases, leaving the description field blank indicates that the exemption certificate will apply to all purchases made by the buyer for the listed seller. Be sure to check the instructions for the form to verify this.

With a **semiblanket or limited exemption,** the buyer is declaring an exemption from transactional taxes for a group of orders placed with the seller for taxable goods and/or services, for example, all orders placed within a specific period of time or all orders placed for specific items or associated with a specific project.

Samples of descriptions are as follows:

o "Materials procured and delivered to jobsite in [city, state]."
o "Materials procured with all purchase orders placed for project number 334422."
o "All purchase orders placed for pipe."

With a **specific exemption or very limited exemption**, the buyer declares exemption from the transactional taxes that may be applicable to a single purchase order or a specific item on a purchase order.

Samples of descriptions are as follows:

- o "Pipe and valves procured on purchase order 334422."
- o "Purchase order 334422."

When issuing an exemption certificate, buyers should consider the following:

1. Whether to issue a blanket exemption, a semiblanket exemption, or a specific declaration.

2. For each exemption type, be sure to use a description that describes everything to which you intend it to apply, nothing more and nothing less.

3. If you issue a blanket or semiblanket certificate, keep track of these, especially if they are subject to expiration. Sometimes, you may find that you have to issue another exemption certificate to replace one that is expiring.

4. If your business strategy changes, you should consider whether this will affect any of the exemption declarations that have been distributed to you. If so, you may have to notify the vendor(s) of the expiration or retraction of the exemption and/or, when applicable, issue a replacement exemption certificate.

Emphasis: For each exemption certificate, make sure that the description and its applicability is appropriate for the exemption declaration.

RECORDKEEPING RESPONSIBILITIES

All parties dealing with exemption certification have some recordkeeping responsibilities as exemption declarations involve legal documents and should be treated as such. Exemption certificates and related documents must be retained and be retrievable as long as required by the tax laws and/or business contracts. They must be presented when requested by a tax auditor or when needed to respond to any other legal request. In effect, the responsibility to keep records on exemption certificates is of similar importance to keeping records of any other legal documents.

When considering storage methods and sites, be sure to choose one that will allow you to retrieve a legible copy in a timely manner. Also, be sure that you store these records in such a manner that unexpected events (such as floods or fires) will not impact their retrieval and so that critters are unable to access them and chew them up.

In regard to duration, some tax authorities indicate that three years of record retention is sufficient. However, three years may not suffice, as most tax audits cover a period ranging from three to four years. Less common are audits covering a period of less than three years and those covering a period of more than five years. And depending upon the findings during a review, tax auditors are able to expand an audit period.

Another consideration when determining how long to retain your records is the time required for the review and analysis phase of an audit. You will find that even though the majority of tax audits deal with a span of three to four years, you should add time for the review and analysis phase. This may easily add another year or two for which you may need to access your records. I know of some audits where the audit was expanded to more than nine years. Therefore, it behooves the recordkeeper to retain his or her records for *at least* six or seven years.

Lastly, do not forget about anything in the business-related contracts requiring you to retain the records longer than statutorily mandated.

Tip: It would be wise to keep records for seven years at a minimum.

INDUSTRY-SPECIFIC EXEMPTIONS

As briefly described earlier, most tax authorities have authorized exemptions for specific industries and some of their activities. There are different reasons for these exemptions, but the primary one is to encourage the growth of the industry or to encourage businesses to move to the region. These, as is the case with any other exemption, are subject to change.

Specific exemptions forms that have been designed for most industry-specific exemption declarations are made available to the public by the issuing tax authority via its website or authorized representative(s). The buyer must use these forms when he or she intends to take advantage of one of these exemptions. If the buyer fails to use the appropriate form, then the tax auditor may not recognize or accept the exemption.

Emphasis: Be sure to use the appropriate exemption certification forms.

Some tax authorities may require that a business complete an application and have it approved and formally authorized to conduct business before the business may claim a specific exemption. Until this application is approved, the exemption will not be valid. Therefore, sellers should check the validity of these exemption certificates.

In general, industrial-based exemptions may be grouped as follows:

| Industrial | Entity type | Goods |
| Service | Tax agreements | Other |

Tax authorities will provide exemptions for some, if not all, of these groupings. The extent of each exemption will depend upon the interest of the taxing authority in attracting businesses to its jurisdictions and thereby raising revenues. Buyers and sellers should be familiar with the different exemptions offered and understand their applicability and/or scope.

See chapter 5 for more information on industries and related exemptions.

Following are brief descriptions of each industry-based exemption:

Industry-based exemptions are available for businesses that either manufacture products, sell tangible products, or provide services for real property. Some examples include the following:

- agriculture
- construction
- energy generation
- farming and ranching
- refineries
- retailers
- wholesalers.

Service-based exemptions are available for businesses that primarily provide services and expertise. Some examples include the following:

- transportation
- communications
- education
- health-care providers
- professionals (examples: engineers, inspectors)
- authorized buyers and mandataries.

Entity-based exemptions are designed to provide exemptions on transactions by entities that are specifically targeted for these exemptions. Some examples include the following:

- governments
- energy providers
- utility providers
- research and development entities
- charities or nonprofits
- fundraising outfits.

Tax agreement–based exemptions are designed to provide exemptions on transactions by entities that have entered into agreements with other taxing authorities. These include the following:

- imports/exports
- international agreements
- intrastate agreements
- interstate agreements.

Other-based exemptions are designed for those businesses that qualify based on specific criteria. This type of exemption may be available in addition to the regular exemption(s) applicable to the business's activities. Some examples are as follows:

- aircrafts
- authorized purchase agent
- direct payment permit exemption
- emergency, natural disaster
- enterprise zones
- foreign purchaser
- high business impact
- Native Americans
- inventory
- occasional sales
- off-road fuels
- maquiladoras
- pollution and environment.

Note: A direct pay permit exemption is available for use only by a business that has been approved for a direct pay permit, which is issued to businesses with a large volume of purchases. It enables the business to pay the taxes directly to the taxing authority instead of to the seller.

NONTAXED GOODS AND SERVICES

Some goods and services are not taxed because they are recognized to provide societal benefits. Most taxing entities have created similar lists of nontaxed goods and services. Other entities will include or exclude some items.

Some things that are more commonly defined as being nontaxed are as follows:

Goods
- medical supplies and equipment
- medicines
- grocery foods.

Services
- medical
- installation
- shipping
- charity.

Taxpayers should keep in mind that some of these nontaxed goods and/or services may become taxable when procured under certain conditions and/or when procured with taxable goods. For those situations, the taxpayer should consider whether an exemption may be applied.

PASS-THROUGH EXEMPTIONS

Some tax entities allow the use of pass-through or flow-through exemptions in certain situations. Pass-through exemptions may be used by an authorized purchasing agent who has been employed by a buyer. This agent will be able to make purchases on behalf of the buyer and will be allowed to use the exemptions that the buyer is entitled to declare. The agent and buyer should formally declare their relationship by signing an agreement or use form, both of which are made available by tax entities.

Other pass-through exemptions may be used when a buyer provides his or her seller with an exemption certificate that is designed to be used by the seller when procuring items or services to be used for the completion of the deliverables to the buyer. This is more commonly used by contractors and subcontractors who are working in chemical plants or refineries in certain states.

Each tax entity will identify the minimum requirements for using a pass-through exemption and its limitations. This usually involves completing forms and/or documents in order to formally appoint the purchasing agent and the seller. The buyer may have to provide a specific exemption form to the seller. The seller may have to meet certain requirements. With this in mind, each participant should be sure the other participant is eligible to take advantage of a pass-through exemption.

EXEMPTIONS AVAILABLE FOR INTERNATIONAL TRADE

Governments have come to recognize that it is imperative that they enable and protect their constituents who do business at the international level. To accomplish this, nations have moved to (1) address the burden of double taxation, which sometimes happens to constituents who participate in international trade; (2) level the field of competition so favoritism is minimized and equality among traders is maximized;

and (3) enable and facilitate the international trade business. Tools to achieve these goals include lobbying, tax treaties, trade agreements, customs requirements for importing and exporting, and declarations and reporting requirements. All of these factors affect applicable taxes, surcharges, and fees, along with reporting requirements.

International tax treaties and trade agreements are enacted by nations in order to address trade and the treatment of taxes and fees that are imposed upon the trade between constituents of two or more nations. The biggest reasons for these agreements are to minimize double taxation, minimize tax evasion, and encourage business activity between the participating nations with a minimum of obstacles. These agreements may or may not have limited life spans and will be modified as needed. However, as a buyer or seller, you would be wise to know whether your transaction is affected by an international trade agreement or tax treaty and, if so, for how long and what impact it may make on the transactions.

A tax treaty and a trade agreement are both known by different names, such as tax treaty, free trade agreement, and trade pact. Trade agreements differ from our domestic reciprocal trade agreements in that the participating parties operate at the national tier and the agreement affects international trade, as opposed to being intrastate or between local jurisdictions.

These agreements are written and governed by international law. The method of enforcement is defined within the agreement, and if the parties are unable to resolve any issues that may arise, they may have to refer the matter to an international organization that has the authority to resolve the matter.

Prior to initiating international trade, or when you intend to do so, you should identify any applicable trade agreements and learn how these will impact your transactions.

Trade agreements define and address different components, including the following:

1. applicable jurisdictions;

2. the type of tax, which may be a transactional tax, an income tax, and/or an inheritance tax;

3. tariff rates and their applicability;

4. possible exemptions and their limitations;

5. support by and for the participating nation(s) when needed in the enforcement of taxes; and

6. mechanisms for dispute resolution.

One of your tasks as an international trader is to identify what taxes apply to your transaction(s). You should not ignore tax treaties, trade agreements, etc. Learn what taxes are imposed, which of these may be reduced or exempted, how the taxes are to be remitted, and any other requirements. To accomplish this, you may have to research another nation's tax laws in order to understand the requirements and/or hire professionals such as customs brokers or tax consultants.

Customs duties and other such charges are levied upon imported and exported goods by the customs authority of the given nation. Some nations use customs duties as a means to control the flow of goods, especially restrictive and prohibited goods, into and out of their borders. These charges are usually not exempted.

Each country has a customs agency or authority that manages the importation and exportation of goods, along with the collection of tariffs. This agency is usually established to monitor and enforce any tax treaties or trade agreements.

Import/export forms and related documents are used to describe, declare, and process the goods that are being imported or exported. Presenting the appropriate documentation, along with any exemption declarations, at the border is a requirement.

These documents contain descriptions of any item(s) being imported or exported, quantities, buyers, sellers, value of the goods, destination, and purpose or intended use. Another purpose of these documents is to substantiate tax liability and any exemption declarations.

Sellers and buyers may use customs brokers to help complete these documents and/or facilitate the processing of the documents. However, the seller may complete some of the documents and submit them to the appropriate agency.

SUMMARY

Sellers and buyers have multiple tax-related responsibilities and must determine whether any transactional taxes apply to their transactions. And when applicable, sellers must either collect from the buyer the properly completed exemption certificates or bill the buyer for the appropriate transactional taxes and remit these to the tax authorities.

Buyers have the responsibility of paying taxes or using tax exemptions. Buyers should research and take advantage of all available exemptions when possible. However, buyers are not required to take advantage of tax exemptions.

Tax exemption declarations must be documented, and the documents must be retained, as required by tax law. All relevant forms must be signed by an authorized representative. It is important to understand that taxing authorities or auditors will not accept a verbal exemption declaration.

Note: Examples of tax forms, including those for exemption certification, are found in the appendix.

Chapter 5

More Industry-Specific Considerations

As briefly mentioned before, tax authorities recognize that different industries may offer different economic benefits to their jurisdictions and that some industries are more beneficial to their constituents than others. Thus, tax authorities enact laws to encourage these industries to do business in their jurisdiction and/or move the business to their jurisdiction.

One of these encouragements is in the form of tax exemptions and/or reduced tax rates. These exemptions may apply to specific purchases, specific sales, or the procurement of specific items. However, some of these encouragements may involve limitations based on value, location, and/or time. And when the tax authorities recognize that it is no longer important or necessary to encourage these industries, they will surely consider changes to the tax laws to reflect this change in perception.

Exemptions are more likely to be provided to a public organization than to a private organization. That is, a government entity or its agent will most likely be given the exemption status. Religions and charitable organizations are likely to qualify for exemptions over private businesses. However, consideration is also given to organizations that may be specially designated for an exemption, such as a historical landmark, a nonprofit organization, or an educational or law enforcement association.

Tax authorities have passed laws to authorize exemptions for different industries and/or organizations. The scope and limitations of these exemptions will be described in the laws. For this, sellers and buyers should do some research in order to determine whether their business has been defined as one that is allowed an exemption.

Following are brief descriptions of some industries and some of the approved exemptions, along with related considerations. I chose to include the industries listed because they are industries commonly addressed by most tax authorities. Keep in mind that this is intended as a general overview. The following is not inclusive of all the details associated with the different exemptions or of all the considerations. For more specific details regarding the exemption and its scope, refer to the appropriate tax jurisdiction and its tax laws.

So, following is a list is of industries/businesses that have been granted industry-specific exemptions by different jurisdictions:

- Advertising
- Aircrafts
- Amusement
- Commercial agriculture
- Contactors and construction
- Customs brokers
- Data processing
- Educational institutions
- Enterprise zones
- Environmental and conservation services
- Fabrication

- Government entities or agencies
- Imports and exports
- Lodging and accommodations
- Manufacturing
- Medicine and health care
- Mining
- Nonprofit organizations
- Public service organizations

- Religious and spiritual organizations
- Rentals and leasing
- Research and development
- Restaurants and food service industry
- Retailers
- Services
- Shipping and delivery
- Telecommunications
- Transportation industry
- Vending devices
- Wholesale

ADVERTISING

The advertising industry is made up of companies that advertise and market products for other companies. Advertisements may be found indoors and outdoors and may be of many different forms. The media used for advertisement include newspapers, periodicals, billboards, and posters. Electronic media include the internet and electronic displays. Other media include broadcast systems and television, both cable and satellite.

Certain jurisdictions may exempt advertising activities. The servicing of any advertising media may also be exempted from sales taxes available in certain jurisdictions, but there may be no exemptions available on the purchase of materials and equipment used to produce the advertisement, so these, in effect, will be taxable. Therefore, if you work in the advertisement industry or use advertising services, check for exemptions and/or identify what is not taxable and, of course, what is taxable.

AIRCRAFTS

Tax authorities define an aircraft as an airplane, helicopter, or other machine capable of flight. An aircraft does not necessarily have to be power driven. Aircrafts include fixed-wing aircraft, with qualifiers, as well as helicopters and airplane flight simulation training devices that are approved by the Federal Aviation Administration. However, different tax authorities may define aircrafts differently as they may specifically exclude devices such as rockets and missiles.

Exemptions are generally available for sales of aircraft to buyers who are in the business of transporting persons or property, or to those who use the aircraft for certain activities associated with agricultural. Exemptions are also available for aircrafts sold to a foreign government and for sales in which the aircraft will be used and registered in another state. But these exemptions may come with exceptions or qualifiers, such as when the first use of the aircraft for flight training and/or the transport of the aircraft out of state.

There are some exemptions available for the repair, remodeling, and maintenance of aircraft(s). This may also extend to include aircraft parts or engines. And some exemptions are available for the purchase of the machinery, tools, supplies, and equipment exclusively used or consumed in the repair, remodeling, or maintenance of the aircraft, its engines, or its parts by persons defined to be able to take advantage of the exemptions.

AMUSEMENT

The amusement industry is known to provide services that entertain or create a diversion for its audience. This industry uses different means or platforms to deliver its services, which vary, as do the providers. Some of the means or platforms used are shows, public fairs, exhibitions, and music concerts. For some of these services, exemptions are available.

Certain types of entertainment or diversion services qualify for an exemption, whereas others do not. The exemptions available depend upon one or more factors. Usually, amusement services that are considered to be for educational purposes are exempted. However, a service provided for profit such as a music concert, play, opera, or ballet is not considered educational and, thus, no exemption is available.

COMMERCIAL AGRICULTURE

Commercial agricultural production involves the commercial selling of crops and livestock that are produced, harvested, or processed by way of farming or ranching activities. It also includes the selling of wholesale divisions of nurseries and the planting, growing, cultivation, and harvesting of shrubs, flowers, trees, and other plants for wholesale. Farming is also considered to include the planting, cultivating, and harvesting of sod for commercial sale.

Exemptions are available for commercial agricultural activities in most jurisdictions. Some of these exemptions apply to the items used to grow the products, for example, fertilizer, feed, seeds, and pesticides. Other available exemptions apply to the machinery and equipment used in the production activities, for example, fence stretchers, picks, postholes, diggers, scoops, and shovels. Other exempted items include lubricants for farm machinery; repair of and replacement parts for machinery used directly in farm or ranch production; and buildings and other structures used in agricultural production.

Activities that may not be considered farming or ranching, and to which the exemptions do not apply, include the operation of greenhouses and plant nurseries, catfish raising, and beekeeping. Neither will any exemptions apply to the ownership of livestock that are used for personal use or pleasure as these are not considered agricultural. Examples include pets and raising horses for pleasure or trail riding, participation in horse shows, or horse racing.

CONTRACTORS AND CONSTRUCTION

Contractors are those who construct or build new structures onto real property. They may also remove and/or replace permanently installed materials to expand an existing structure. The structures and/or properties that are worked upon are usually classified as industrial, commercial, or residential. Understanding the classification of the properties will help to determine which tax benefits and rates are applicable to the contractor's transactions.

In some states, contractors may issue exemption certificates for the materials they procure and permanently install into the customer's permanent structure. In these states, the contractor is considered a retailer of the materials. In other states, contractors are considered to be the consumers of the permanent incorporated materials and, in effect, are responsible for paying transactional taxes on these materials.

Few states allow the end customer, such as a refinery or a manufacturer, to provide its contractor with a pass-through exemption so the contractor may provide it to his or her seller(s) to declare the exemption or reduce the transactional taxes charged on materials. Look for this and be wary of limitations.

When contractors bill their customers for their taxable services, they are required also to bill for applicable sales taxes unless the buyer provides valid exemption documentation.

Some states will impose a "contractor's" tax upon the revenue earned by the contractor instead of imposing sales taxes upon the buyer of the contractor's services. Some of these states allow the contractor to directly bill the customer for the reimbursement of this contractor tax, whereas others do not. In such cases where the contractor is not able to directly pass the cost on, he or she has to absorb this as part of his or her overhead costs.

Other states allow the end customer, such as a refinery, to submit a request for reimbursement of any taxes paid by the contractor on materials that were permanently installed and for which the end customer reimbursed the contractor.

When requesting contractor services, industrial customers should consider whether the project is a repair, new construction, add-on construction, an improvement, remodeling, or regularly scheduled maintenance. Each of these activities may be treated differently by the tax authority.

Contractors should look for exemptions issued by tax authorities such as those for enterprise zones and manufacturers. Customers should consider whether their property is in a specially designated area that is also subject to tax exemptions or tax rate discounts. See the section on enterprise zones for more information.

CUSTOMS BROKERS

Customs brokers are private entities such as private individuals, partnerships, or corporations who are licensed, regulated, and empowered by United States Customs and Border Protection (CBP) to provide services to importers and exporters of goods. Brokers are responsible for assisting their customers, the importers and exporters, and ensuring they meet the federal requirements imposed upon their import and export activities. Brokers are also responsible for submitting to CBP the necessary information and documents and the appropriate payments on behalf of their clients. In turn, the customs brokers charge a fee to their clients for their services and the reimbursement of costs incurred by the customs broker.

A customs broker must be registered with states or tax jurisdictions in order to take advantage of any exemptions to the sales taxes imposed on goods, exported or imported. The broker will likely be required to pay a license fee, which will allow him or her to issue a certificate of export to be used for the declaration of exemption from sales taxes on the goods to be exported. The brokers are also responsible for ensuring the completion of required forms for any exemption declarations and for the processing and remittance of taxes and fees imposed on the goods, as well as issuing any refunds.

See the section titled "Imports and Exports" for related information.

DATA PROCESSING

Data processing is a service that includes data entry, word processing, data search/retrieval, information compilation, and accounting data reproduction. It most likely involves the use of a computer for entering and processing the data. When considering data processing, look to determine whether other, related services are excluded from this category, such as medical transcription, which is not considered data processing.

Some jurisdictions consider data processing to be a taxable service and will allow an exemption from tax on a portion of the sales price. One such jurisdiction is the state of Texas, which allows a 20 percent exemption on the amount billed. So, if the service provider bills you $1,000 for data processing services, the taxable amount will be 80 percent of the $1,000, which is $800. In this case, if the tax rate is 8.25 percent and the amount billed is $1,000, then the tax amount will be calculated by following these steps:

1	Determine the taxable amount.	Multiply the amount billed by 80 percent. ($800 = $1,000 × 0.80)
2	Determine the tax amount.	Multiply the taxable amount by the tax rate. ($66 = $800 × 0.0825)

Taxpayers should look for exemptions on machinery and equipment used by persons or entities that are primarily engaged in providing computer services and data processing. Some of these exempted items may include barcode readers, computers, plotters, printers, software, memory, and servers. Usually, these types of exemptions will not include consumables such as computer cleaning products, paper, pens, and labels.

Taxpayers should not confuse a business's use of computers and/or computer-related equipment for providing data processing services to its customers with a business's use of such equipment for the purpose of managing its own accounting records, sales, purchases, etc. There is a difference. Basically, one may be considered to be the tools and equipment needed to produce the business's products/services, whereas the other is used as an office tool and therefore is most likely taxable.

EDUCATIONAL INSTITUTIONS

Educational institutions are considered public service providers and may be financed by public and/or private entities. If the financing comes from a public source, the source is generally a governmental entity that collects taxes such as property taxes from taxpayers. Privately financed institutions usually charge tuition, fees, and surcharges. Both types of institutions may accept contributions or grants in order to help cover costs, offer scholarships, and/or provide other student aid to their customers (i.e., students).

The exemptions available to educational institutions may apply to the goods and services procured and used for the purpose of providing the service. These exemptions, along with any limitations, vary according to the taxing authorities of the jurisdiction.

From the perspective of the service recipients (i.e., students), exemptions usually do not apply to any of the products or supplies the recipients procure to use with the services. But when exemptions are provided for these items, they will likely be limited, such as tax holidays on school-related supplies, clothing, and shoes, or exemptions available to some students with defined disabilities or who meet special conditions.

ENTERPRISE ZONES

Enterprise zones are geographical areas where economic growth and development are encouraged by governments via the use of investment incentives, reduced regulations, and tax laws. The primary beneficiaries of these incentives are businesses that invest in enterprise zones and adhere to the requirements thereof. Usually, these zones are marked by an absence of economic development or have faltered in terms of their economic status, hence the perceived need to encourage business activity in these areas.

The federal program that established enterprise zones also calls them empowerment zones, enterprise communities, and renewal communities. Different tiers of government establish and manage different enterprise zones, which may be known as urban enterprise zones, development enterprise zones, or economic development zones. Businesses that are located in an enterprise zone should research whether they qualify for any of the available benefits.

Some zones may include the proper name of the government, such as the following:

- Virginia Enterprise Zone
- Douglas County Enterprise Zone
- Chicago Enterprise Zone
- Maryland Enterprise Zone (MEZ).

In order to take advantage of the benefits, businesses have to complete an application and be approved and thereby formally recognized. A business should check with its local chamber of commerce and tax authorities, which may have a website with information on enterprise zones. Businesses should also research whether they may share their exemption status with their sellers to take advantage of the available benefits and minimize costs for all.

Sellers who sell to buyers who are located in these zones should check whether each buyer has been certified as a business that qualifies for the benefits. If so certified, the buyer may be able to provide exemption certificates that are not normally available elsewhere; may have pass-through exemption certification for the seller to use; or may provide the documentation the seller needs to apply for exemption certification.

ENVIRONMENTAL AND CONSERVATION SERVICES

Environmental and conservation services are intended to protect environments, habitats, and animal life-forms from any loss, damage, or destruction resulting from the actions of human beings and to protect and enhance trees, vegetation, soil, animals, water quality, and air quality, with other targets being waste management and environmental management. The services are also intended to educate and to implement energy conservation practices where possible.

There are various methods and tools used to support the goals of environmental protection and energy conservation. Activities may include construction of dams, restocking of lakes with fishes, cleaning up oil spills, and minimizing or eliminating air pollution. Supporting activities include scientific research, lobbying, and enactment of laws and policies. Government agencies and nonprofit agencies have been established to enforce laws related to environmental protection and energy conservation and to accomplish other related goals.

With the aforementioned in mind, exemptions are made available for different activities related to environmental protection and energy conservation, but these may have some limitations imposed, such as a percentage of the costs paid for services related to environmental protection or energy conservation. Each tax authority will describe the items that qualify for the exemption and will define the time period in which the sales may occur.

Some of these exemptions may apply to items such as the following:

- Repair, remodeling, maintenance, or restoration that is required by the government to protect the environment or to conserve energy.

  Note: These exemptions may have some limitations, such as being applicable to the materials billed only when the associated labor is billed separately.

- Pollution control devices and systems.
- Energy- and water-efficient products when the sale occurs in a specified time period as described by the relevant tax authority.
- Water and wastewater systems, including equipment used to recycle and reuse harvested rainwater.
- Equipment, services, or supplies used solely to construct or operate a water and wastewater system certified by a government agency.
- Costs associated with the reuse or recycling of wastewater that will be used in fracturing work performed for an oil or gas well, or for equipment and services.
- Supplies used for desalination of surface water or ground water or other such environmental services.

FABRICATION

Fabrication is the process of constructing or manufacturing a new product using raw and/or prepared components. Fabrication may be for customized or specialty products that likely involve metal components. Fabrication is usually performed in a shop where needed machinery, tools, equipment, supplies, and materials are readily available.

Fabricators may use one or more of a number of different platforms to sell their products. They may choose to sell their products at retail or wholesale. Or they may provide installation services along with the products they sell.

When the fabricator sells his fabricated product without installing it, he is basically selling at retail or wholesale. For this, the fabricator should request and collect an exemption certificate from the buyer or charge any applicable taxes.

When the fabricator sells the fabricated product with installation services, she needs to consider into what the product will be installed. If the fabricator permanently installs her product into real property, then she may be considered to be performing contractor services. If the fabricated product is installed into another item and it stays in the form of a tangible personal product, then the fabricator will likely have to treat this sale as retail or a repair.

Generally, the fabricator's purchasing department may be able to declare an exemption from transactional taxes on the materials the fabricator procures that become part of the fabricated product. However, the fabricator should check to determine whether he will be able to declare an exemption for any consumables, tools, or other things he uses in the fabrication process.

Buyers of the fabricated products will have to determine both the tax status of the purchased item and whether they may take advantage of any exemptions.

If the fabricated product is for exportation, the seller/buyer may use the export documentation to support any exemption declaration for the items exported out of the sourcing tax jurisdiction. Buyers may also use these documents to identify what taxes have been paid and/or to determine whether use taxes are or are not due on the imported items.

GOVERNMENT ENTITIES OR AGENTS

Government entities and government agencies include the United States and its subtiers, as described in prior chapters. Government entities may also include an unincorporated instrumentality of the United States, or an agency that is owned by the United States or by a corporation that is owned by the United States.

For the most part, sales, rentals, and/or leases made to a government entity may be deemed exempt from transactional taxes. The seller or lessor may also be able to declare an exemption from paying taxes on the storage, use, or consumption of a taxable item. So, if you are selling, renting, or leasing a taxable item to a government entity, you may expect to receive an exemption certificate indicating that the buyer is a government entity or government agency.

IMPORTS AND EXPORTS

Services provided for the importation or exportation of goods are usually performed by a customs broker or his or her authorized agent. The sellers/buyers of the goods to be exported or imported may also be able to complete and process some of the documents that the brokers usually handle. Keep in mind, however, that certain transactions are more efficiently performed by a customs broker, who can complete the paperwork and manage the process.

Importers/exporters will have to complete documentation that adheres to government regulations. These documents are used to declare the items, state their value, and provide other information. Once the paperwork is certified, the associated fees, taxes, and surcharges will be determined and then will have to be paid.

Most brokers will pay any excise taxes, import/export taxes, and related surcharges and fees. Of course, these costs will be passed on to the broker's customer. The taxes imposed upon the buyer's goods must be listed separately and properly labeled on the customer's invoices.

Sellers may use the export documentation to support the exemptions available for the items being exported from the sourcing tax jurisdiction. Buyers may use these documents to identify what taxes have been paid and/or to support or identify use taxes due or not due. Overall, all parties should keep copies of all the import/export documents as required by law and/or contract.

See the section titled "Customs Brokers" for related information.

LODGING AND ACCOMMODATIONS

Lodging and accommodations involves the rental or leasing of a dwelling, room, or other transient accommodation to travelers. The tax imposed is generally labeled as an occupancy fee or something similar. These taxes vary according to jurisdiction and may be imposed at the local and state level and at different rates.

Some jurisdictions eliminate the rental tax when the duration of the rental of the lodging or accommodation exceeds a defined duration, such as twenty-eight or thirty consecutive days. When this duration is exceeded, the rentee should check to ensure that the renter no longer bills the rental tax when it no longer applies.

Another consideration for these buyers is the difference between the rental or lease of a lodging or accommodation for a traveler versus the rental or lease of housing. Lodging is a room that is rented to a traveler for the purpose of sleeping and living in. A transient accommodation is a dwelling or living quarter that is rented to a traveler for sleeping and living in for a period of time. Lodging and accommodation structures generally include hotels, inns, motels, and cruise ships, whereas housing may involve an apartment, a house, or a condominium.

MANUFACTURING

Manufacturing is the large-scale production of tangible personal property or the conversion or conditioning of tangible personal property into a different form, composition, quality, or character with the use of labor, machines, tools, and/or chemical or biological processes. This mostly applies to the industrial or commercial transformation of raw materials into a finished good.

Exemptions are available to manufacturers, although these exemptions may vary based on the industry. For example, refineries may have exemptions or tax rates different from those of chemical manufacturers. Exemptions are available for procured goods that are incorporated into the finished goods. Exemptions are also available for some manufacturing machinery and equipment, and the replacement of parts that are used in the manufacturing activities. Some exemptions are offered for some preventive maintenance activities.

Exemptions may not apply to all the manufacturer's tools, equipment, and transport mediums. Some jurisdictions offer exemptions for some gases, fuels, and lubricants used during the manufacturing process, whereas others do not offer these exemptions.

Taxpayers should look for other exemptions that may be available for activities such as the construction of new manufacturing facilities or the expansion of existing manufacturing capacities, special enterprise zones, or other special interests.

MEDICAL AND HEALTH-CARE INDUSTRY

The medical and health-care industry strives to provide people with preventive, curative, rehabilitative, therapeutic, and/or other palliative remediation of a physical, mental, and/or emotional condition. Included in this industry are institutions such as hospitals, clinics, rehabilitation centers, diagnostic laboratories, pathology clinics, and residential health facilities. The service providers include doctors, nurses, therapists, and other professionals, along with support staff. Part of this industry includes the sales and use of products such as medicine, medical equipment, and appliances. As you may have envisioned, this is a vast industry that covers a lot of activities.

Most tax authorities do not tax certain medical-related services as these are considered public services. But because some of the services and products provided involve the commercialization of such, some of the items are taxed. To determine which these are, look at how the tax authorities classify the products and services. Also look for exemptions available for the goods and services used by health-care providers to provide their own goods and services to their patients and clients. Do not forget to identify nontaxed medical and health-care-related items.

As a general rule, tax authorities do not tax products that are prescribed as medical treatment by licensed professionals, such as medical doctors. Some examples of nontaxed products are medical drugs, prosthetic devices, and inpatient treatments. On the other hand, products that are not prescribed by medical doctors, such as over-the-counter drugs, will likely be taxed.

MINING

The mining industry involves the process of extracting ores, precious minerals, and other geological raw materials from the earth. Mining activities include geological and environmental analysis, managing environmental impacts resulting from the mining activities, and the acquisition and use of specialized equipment and machinery.

Some tax authorities require miners to register, acquire permits, and gain other formal certification to be formally acknowledged and approved to conduct business. In effect, miners should verify that their mining operations qualify as such in order to take advantage of any available tax exemptions or discounts.

Exemptions are available for miners whose operations are intended to profit from commercial and industrial activities. In other words, these exemptions will not apply to operations carried out for personal use, such as when engaging in a hobby, or where the miners make personal use of the ores they mine. Do look for limitations on any exemption.

The exemptions available for mining operations are basically production based, exempting and/or discounting the taxes associated with the costs of machinery, equipment, tools, accessories, and other items that are used to carry out the operation. These exemptions may differ depending on which ore or mineral is being mined, which tax jurisdiction the operation falls under, and other criteria. The documents and forms required to declare the exemptions will likely vary between tax jurisdictions too.

NONPROFIT ORGANIZATIONS

Nonprofit organizations are entities that have been granted tax-exempt status by the Internal Revenue Service (IRS) because they provide a public benefit or support a social cause. See IRS Code sections 501(a) and 501(c)(4) for further information. Examples of nonprofit organizations include hospitals, universities, charities, churches, and foundations.

Nonprofit organizations must serve the public and promote social welfare through the offering of either goods or services (or both). More importantly, these organizations are *not* to be used for the personal gain or benefit of their founders, employees, supporters, relatives, and/or associates.

Generally, exemptions are available to a registered nonprofit organization for taxes related to the procurement of the services and/or goods the organization uses to provide its own services and/or goods. These exemptions and their limitations may vary depending on the different taxing authorities.

PUBLIC SERVICE ORGANIZATIONS

Public service organizations are entities established with a goal of serving all the members of the communities that they have defined as the beneficiaries of their services. These entities are usually government based and offer their services directly or indirectly to the beneficiaries. Examples include the public education system, police, firefighters, paramedics, social services, military forces, mail delivery, public transportation, waste management, utility providers, and courts.

Governmental public service providers are financed by taxes and by contributions made or charges paid by the recipients or buyers of the service. On the other hand, privately owned public service organizations are predominantly financed by the monies paid by the recipients or buyers of the service.

Exemptions are generally available to public service providers for items and goods they procure for providing their services and will vary (as will their limitations) depending on the taxing authority.

RELIGIOUS AND SPIRITUAL ORGANIZATIONS

A religious or spiritual-based organization must be registered with the IRS as a nonprofit organization and/or be able demonstrate it is not for profit before it may advertise itself as a provider of religious or spiritual services. Such an organization engages primarily in operating a religious institution such as a church, temple, or monastery and also administrates and/or promotes an organized religion and/or spiritual activities.

Exemptions are generally available to a registered religious or spiritual organization for the services and/or goods it may procure for use in providing its own services and goods. These exemptions may vary with the taxing authorities, as may the limitations.

From the perspective of a customer of these entities, exemptions generally do *not* apply to any products procured for use along with some of the services offered.

RENTALS AND LEASING

Rental and leasing is where a payment is made for the use of a property. Most states consider rentals to be a defined number of days in duration, usually less than twenty-eight or thirty. When the rental exceeds this duration, it is considered to be a lease and its tax rate may be reduced.

Most states have a rental/lease tax imposed upon the rentee/lessee. However, some states impose the rental/lease tax upon the renter/lessor (seller), who in turn may pass this on to the buyer as a pass-through cost.

Taxes on rentals or leases are calculated based upon the gross income generated from the rental or lease. Surcharges and fees may be imposed on the transaction too. This will depend upon what is rented or leased and where. Also, the rental/lease tax rate may vary from the standard sales tax rate as it is defined as a separate transactional tax.

Both buyers and sellers should also be cognizant of additional fees, surcharges, and taxes imposed upon the rental or lease of a certain property. Some of these include hazmat fees, an emissions reduction fee, and a heavy equipment tax. Other charges may include pass-through costs such as property or inventory taxes imposed upon the owner of the property.

Another consideration relevant to the rental/lease tax is when equipment is rented with an operator. Under certain circumstances, both the rented equipment and the labor of the operator may be taxable. Other times, the transaction will be considered a service and may be nontaxable. When determining whether the transaction is a rental or a service, you should start by identifying who exercises direct control over or supervises the operator of the rented property. If the buyer does not exercise direct control over or supervise the operator, then it is likely considered a service. Another consideration is whether the intent of the transaction is to rent or lease the equipment and separately furnish the operator. Both parties should be aware of how the laws are written for these types of rentals.

RESEARCH AND DEVELOPMENT

Research and development involves activities whose ultimate goal is to produce a new product and/or service so it may be marketed, sold, and/or used to improve existing products and/or services. Staff members may include engineers, scientists, researchers, laboratory technicians, and support staff. Industries that normally engage in research and development activities include pharmaceuticals, semiconductors, and technology.

Considerations for sales tax exemptions include whether the research and development activities are recognized as a business expense, whether they are part of a cooperative joint venture, and/or whether they have been specifically defined as nontaxable. If the activities are part of the business's normal expenses, chances are slim that there are any applicable exemptions. However, if the activities are recognized as part of a joint venture, some exemptions may be available.

RESTAURANTS AND FOOD SERVICE INDUSTRY

The restaurant and food service industry includes any establishment that prepares, serves, and/or delivers food or food products to its customers. These establishments include restaurants, fast-food providers, cafeterias, dining halls, vending companies, hotels and inns, and anywhere else food or food products are sold. In general, the activities of restaurants and the food service industry are commercial in nature, as opposed to foods sold at retail to customers for their personal preparation and consumption.

The two most predominant activities of these industries are (1) food preparation and serving/delivery and (2) food production and distribution. Other related activities involve supplying equipment and any services needed by the food providers. Food preparation and service usually includes the employment of waitstaff, hosts, bartenders, busboys, chefs, cooks, managers, and support staff who enable the serving and/or delivery of the foods and beverages. Food producers and distributors include farmers and ranchers. The suppliers of food-related equipment and services usually include food and beverage warehouses, distributors, and salespeople who support this activity.

Some of the goods and services procured to prepare, sell, and/or serve foods and beverages at retail may be taxable, such as a service charge included in the price of a meal served in a restaurant, whereas a loaf of bread sold for take-out may be nontaxable. It depends on how each tax authority defines food and food-related service. In general, nonprocessed goods are not taxable, whereas processed foods that are served are usually taxable (with the end consumer being the one to pay the tax).

For this industry, look for the definition of goods that are considered as foods versus the definition of goods considered to be nonfoods, the latter of which are likely taxable. Examples of nonfood products include alcohol and tobacco products. Examples of nontaxable meals include meals furnished to staff and students of educational institutions, staff members and patients of hospitals, and inmates and patients of mental institutions. Also, some customers may be able to declare an exemption for the foods procured, but this usually depends upon the end use of such foods.

RETAILERS

A retailer sells goods to a buyer who is the ultimate consumer or user of those goods. Retail sales do not involve sales to customers who buy the goods for resale, manufacturing, fabrication, or other commercial purposes. Retail sales usually exclude sales made to nonprofit and governmental entities.

Retail formats used by retailers include brick-and-mortar retail sites (stores), websites, marketplaces, flea markets, and telephone sales.

Most jurisdictions define retail activities as those involving participants such as brokers or agents who are authorized to sell, lease, or rent property on behalf of the product/property owner. Such a person may also be known as a cashier or salesperson (among other job titles).

Most jurisdictions exclude the occasional seller from its definition of a retailer, meaning that the occasional seller's transaction(s) may not be taxable. Occasional sellers are those who do not regularly engage, or hold themselves to be engaged, in the business of selling items at retail. Occasional sales are usually limited by the number of sales completed within a set time period, such as one or two sales of taxable items within a twelve-month period.

Look for the tax authority to declare a person or business to be a retailer or to be engaged in retail business within its jurisdiction when a seller has established a footprint in that jurisdiction. Evidence of an established footprint includes the maintenance, occupation, or use of an office, distribution center, salesroom or sample room, warehouse, or storage facility, or operation or completion of activities via a representative, agent, salesperson, canvasser, or solicitor who operates within the jurisdiction.

Exemptions that are applicable to the retail sales depend on the applicable tax laws, a buyer's basis for declaring an exemption, the buyer's tax status, and so forth. Retailers may issue a resale exemption certificate for items procured for resale. Look for other applicable exemptions.

Retailers, as sellers, are usually held responsible for the billing and collection of applicable taxes from the buyer. Afterward, the retailer must remit the accrued taxes to the appropriate tax authority.

SERVICES

Services are actions or work that is performed for a buyer in exchange for some consideration or value. Services are performed by different classes of service providers, such as professionals, tradespeople, and personal consumption service providers. Some jurisdictions and/or government agencies require certain service providers to be licensed and/or registered with the appropriate tax authorities or professional organizations before they may provide their services.

Professional service providers are usually licensed or certified by governmental or other authorized agencies that oversee the profession. Licensed professionals include certified accountants, lawyers, medical professionals, engineers, and inspectors.

Some of the services provided may be taxable; some are not taxable; and some may be eligible for tax discounts or exemptions. Note, though, that services performed for purposes of personal consumption are usually taxable, including lawn care, cleaning, and barber and hair-related services.

In general, the buyer should check with the tax jurisdiction to learn what is taxable or exempt and under what condition(s). Also, the buyer should consider that some states impose a tax on sellers for services sold, and this tax may be visibly passed on to the buyer as a separate line item on an invoice. At this time, these states include Hawaii and New Mexico. Other considerations include whether exempt entities are involved in providing the service.

SHIPPING AND DELIVERY

Shipping and delivery is a service used to transfer the possession of tangible goods between two parties. Sellers who are responsible for arranging the shipment and delivery of the goods will either use their own transportation or hire a third-party carrier to complete the delivery. Third-party carriers include USPS, FedEx, and UPS, among other common carriers that provide said services to their customers. The scheduled shipping date will be based upon an agreed upon delivery date. However, if the buyer arranges for the pickup of the goods from the seller, the customer will either use his or her own transportation or hire a third-party carrier to pick up the goods and deliver them to the destination designated by the buyer.

Some tax authorities consider the costs billed to the buyer for the shipping and delivery of goods procured to be part of the cost of the goods. Therefore, if the goods to be shipped are taxable, the related shipping and delivery charges will likely be considered taxable, too. If some of the invoiced goods procured are taxable, the taxes on the associated shipping and delivery costs will be prorated. Conversely, if the goods to be shipped are considered nontaxable, then the related shipping and delivery services billed will be considered nontaxable. In most cases, when buyers declare an exemption on the goods procured, the exemption declaration will extend to include the shipping and delivery charges.

When a buyer hires a third-party carrier to do nothing more than pick up and deliver the goods he or she has procured, these services are generally considered nontaxable. Check with the relevant tax authority to learn its position on this and on related criteria and limits.

Another consideration is that interstate shipping and delivery charges are usually considered a nontaxable service.

TELECOMMUNICATIONS

Telecommunications involve electronics, electrical transmissions, and conveyance of communications using routers, receptions of sounds, signals, data or information utility wires, cable, radio waves, microwaves, satellites, fiber optics, or any other method now in existence or that may be devised, including but not limited to telephone services. In general, broadcasts by licensed commercial radio or television stations are regulated by the Federal Communications Commission, with the exception of cable television services.

Certain telecommunication services are taxed, and others are nontaxed. Local taxes may be imposed upon intrastate calls based on where the call originates or, if the origination location is unidentifiable, where the call is billed. One nontaxable situation is a long-distance call that involves an originating service point (caller) that is located in a different state from the receiving point (receiver).

In general, buyers of telecommunication services should be aware that mobile telecommunication services may or may not be exempted. They should also be aware of the different communications-based taxes and the changes thereto. Buyers should take time to familiarize themselves with the service provided, the mediums used, and the terminology used. This should help with understanding the applicable taxes, surcharges, fees, and available exemptions and with the identification of any overcharges.

TRANSPORTATION INDUSTRY

The transportation industry provides a service for the movement of people, goods, and/or animals from one location to a destination, whether this is done over land, through air, and/or over water. The mode of transportation usually includes the use of airlines, railways, ships, cruise liners, automobiles, and trucks. Some businesses are testing the use of drones to deliver products.

There are different considerations to be aware of when identifying the taxability of transportation services. Available exemptions are affected by whether the service offered is predominantly dedicated to the commercial movement of people, goods, and animals. Another consideration is whether the transporter's services involve the use of other goods and/or services from other industries, such as logistics, warehouses, fuel suppliers, or transportation-related infrastructures.

Some states have imposed a tax on transportation service fees for the movement of people, with some exceptions. Generally, tax is not imposed on interstate transportation, public transit systems, medical transportation, or paratransit services. Some states consider animals as tangible personal property, so they treat the transportation of animals similarly to the transportation of goods. Some states follow simple taxing principles, including the following: (1) When a seller bills the buyer for shipping charges to deliver taxable items, the shipping charges are also taxable. (2) When a seller bills the buyer for the delivery of nontaxable or exempted items, the associated shipping charges are not taxed. (3) If the carrier does not provide any other service with the transportation/delivery service, this service is generally nontaxable. Be sure to check with the relevant taxing authorities to verify that these principles apply.

VENDING DEVICES

Vending devices come in different forms and are used to sell different products such as candies, foods, drinks, and items for amusement, which may include music, entertainment, or games. These devices, which may be in the form of a pool table, shuffleboard, or pinball machine, are usually placed in locations where buyers may easily access them and their products. Most of these devices have a feature that allows payments to be made using coins, paper currency, tokens, and/or credit cards, all of which may be inserted into the vending devices.

Yes, transactional taxes are imposed upon these devices and the products sold via these devices. The taxes imposed vary according to the tax authorities, as do any available exemptions. With this in mind, look for variations in the application of these taxes and related responsibilities, including the following:

- Requirement that the owners of the vending devices pay taxes via a permit or via annual fees.

- Definition of certain products and price ranges to which taxes may apply.
- Sales taxes imposed on products that sell for a set amount.
- Sales taxes imposed on part of a product's selling price.
- Specific products are taxed, such as chewing gum, food, and candy.

Exceptions to paying some of these taxes may apply to owners who are a nonprofit organization or a government. And an exception may be made when the devices are stocked and/or maintained by individuals with special needs as part of a skills and education program operated by a nonprofit organization.

Regardless of the vending device type, owner, products sold, and so forth, the owner must maintain accounting records because these are auditable just as with any other business type.

WHOLESALES

Wholesales are sales where goods are sold in large quantities to customers who include retailers, merchants, distributors, or industrial, commercial, or institutional users who, in turn, may use the goods in their manufacturing or business activities. Wholesalers may buy goods in large quantities from the producers or manufacturers, then store them in warehouses, and upon demand sell the goods in smaller quantities to their customers. Many wholesalers are essentially middlemen between manufacturers and buyers.

Wholesalers must be aware of the requirements for tax to be exempted on their purchases. Exemptions are generally available to those businesses that buy goods for resale purposes. Wholesalers may be required to complete an exemption certificate form specifically designed for resale transactions or may be able to use their sales tax permits to declare their exemptions.

SUMMARY

The descriptions in this chapter do not include all industries or every aspect of each industry. I chose them as examples because they are high level and generic, as is the tax-related information. What is included herein may not apply to each tax jurisdiction that is relevant to the industry or to each aspect of the industry. My primary purpose for sharing this information in this format is to inform the reader of what to consider and/or research when trying to understand the treatment of taxes for any transaction within a particular industry.

The most important points to consider are the following:

1. Different industries have different tax responsibilities and exemption considerations.

2. Some items have sales/use taxes imposed upon them, whereas others do not.

3. Some items have special consumption taxes imposed upon them instead of the standards sales and use taxes. These items include fuel, motor oil, cement, alcoholic beverages, motor vehicles, trailers, and insurance premiums.

4. Exemptions are available for some of the imposed transactional taxes.

Emphasis: Sellers and buyers need to consider and research whether the industry, service, or product has been given special consideration in terms of tax exemption.

Chapter 6

Responsibilities Related to Tax Reporting

Taxpayers are held responsible for reporting their taxes to each tax jurisdiction as required. For this, each taxpayer should become familiar with his or her business registrations and transactions, where transactions are completed, and any other activity that may trigger the need for reporting taxes.

The tax reporting process consists of six steps, as follows:

1. Determine when a tax return or report is required.

2. Do data preparation and calculations.

3. Complete the appropriate tax form(s) or use the appropriate reporting tools.

4. Submit tax returns and reports to the relevant tax jurisdictions.

5. Remit payment for tax balances, or address any credits.

6. Keep records.

Tax reporting must be completed when the taxpayer has met the criteria prescribed by each relevant tax authority. Some of these criteria are as follows:

1. when the taxpayer has acquired a sales tax permit;

2. when the taxpayer establishes nexus in the tax jurisdiction;

3. when the taxpayer must report sales, use, or another transactional tax; and/or

4. when the volume of sales exceeds a minimum amount prescribed by the tax authority.

1. DETERMINE WHEN A TAX RETURN OR REPORT IS REQUIRED.

The filing frequency and due dates of tax returns are defined by each tax authority. These will vary among tax authorities and according to the business's activities and volume. Most tax authorities require monthly, quarterly, semiannual, or annual filings. However, the frequency and due dates can be changed based on defined triggering events and situations.

When a business is registered, its agents must identify its filing frequency, which is usually determined based on the anticipated activities and volume of the business. After the filing frequency has been identified, the business must adhere to its filing schedule unless the business triggers a filing frequency change or a tax authority authorizes a special filing frequency.

Taxpayers should be familiar with any triggers that may cause a change to their filing frequency and/or due dates. Factors that commonly trigger a change in filing frequency include changes in the business's average tax liability or its revenue. These triggers may cause the filing frequency to increase from annually to semiannually or decrease from monthly to quarterly. For example, if the revenue amount reported in a prior filing period exceeds the amount bracket defined by the tax authorities for a previously established filing frequency, this will be a triggering event that will cause an increase in the filing frequency. If the reported amounts are lower, the filing frequency may be reduced from monthly to quarterly, from quarterly to semiannually, or from semiannually to annually. If the average tax liability is in the intermediate range, then the filing frequency may be quarterly. Because the tax authorities may change the filing frequency standards, taxpayers should keep this possibility in mind.

When a business is registered, some tax authorities will actually identify the filing frequency for the taxpayer. Some tax authorities will use processes to help identify any triggers that will require a change in the filing frequency of a business. And some tax authorities will proactively notify a business of a change in its frequency via a letter or email. However, if the tax authority does not share this information, the taxpayer must be proactive and identify any change and adhere to it.

As with the filing frequency, the due date for filing a tax return is normally predefined, usually twenty or so days after the end of the reporting period.

Changes to the standard due date are generally not dependent upon the taxpayer's activities or volume. Instead, the changes are made based upon predefined triggers. One common trigger is when the due date falls on a holiday or weekend, which may cause it to be moved to the next business day. Another trigger is an adverse event, such as a natural disaster, for which the tax authority must enact a law or formal declaration to authorize a postponement of the due date.

When a tax jurisdiction decides to change the due date for a tax return or any other reporting requirement, it must complete the legislative process and formally authorize this change. After the change is authorized, the tax authority has the responsibility of notifying affected taxpayers. Taxpayers should be on the alert and look for this, especially if they have been directly affected by a natural disaster or another adverse event.

When a taxpayer does not comply with his or her filing frequency and/or due dates, there are costs and consequences. Late filers have to pay penalties and interest. Another consequence might be the loss of the business license and/or any permits. Also, a history of late reporting is likely to increase the chance that the taxpayer will be selected for a tax audit—and it will extend the statute of limitations on audits by the tax authorities.

Emphasis: Taxpayers need to be sure to know when their tax returns or tax reports are due, and they must adhere to the filing frequency and due dates. Otherwise, they may encounter unwanted consequences.

2. DO DATA PREPARATION AND CALCULATIONS.

In order to adhere to its tax reporting responsibilities, a business should use its accounting information system to generate reports that provide the data needed to populate tax returns. Some businesses have well-designed, sophisticated software programs that easily generate the appropriate reports with the necessary data in a format that will facilitate the reporting for different tax jurisdictions. Other businesses have to generate several reports and/or data extracts in order to collect and prepare all the data necessary to complete their tax returns.

In general, the data needed to complete a sales tax return will include the following items:

- the entity's registration or tax identification number
- address
- contact information
- gross revenue
- taxable revenue
- exempted revenue

- costs
- taxable costs
- exempt costs
- costs by counties or other local-level tiers
- other information.

Most businesses strive to automate the generation of accounting information in a format that will facilitate reporting. Some information systems provide standardized reports. Others allow for the customization of reports. All this is dependent upon the features of the information system, the accounting modules, and how they are configured.

Accounting managers should consider, suggest, and/or request modifications to their accounting software if the appropriate reports are unable to be generated with ease or present information in a user-friendly format. The purpose of this is to minimize the manual handling of data and to maximize the automation of data preparation for the completion of tax returns and reports.

3. COMPLETE THE APPROPRIATE TAX FORM(S) OR USE THE APPROPRIATE REPORTING TOOLS.

Tax forms are designed to be used by taxpayers and tax authorities for tax reporting purposes. Taxpayers will use these forms to comply with their responsibility to report their business activities and calculate any taxes that are either due or refundable. Tax authorities use the returns to analyze taxpayers' business activities and to help identify noncompliance, as well as collect statistical information.

Tax authorities authorize the design and use of their own tax forms. Each of these forms is given an identification number and a name. Some lower-tier tax jurisdictions allow the reporting of taxes by using the forms designed for a higher tier. In effect, a combination of tax jurisdictions may use the same form.

Some tax authorities have developed different tax forms to be used to report different types of business activities and/or taxes. Some may allow the use of the same form for the reporting of the different business activities. Also, some tax returns will require supplemental forms (pages) to enable the submission of all related and relevant data.

The forms that are available for tax reporting generally come in two basic formats: (1) hard copy (printed) and (2) electronic reporting format. The hard copies may be downloaded or printed directly from the tax authority's website, generated by a tax software program, or acquired from authorized representatives. The electronic format will involve the use of the internet and web pages designed for the population and/or uploading of tax data. Of course, uploads must adhere to certain formatting requirements. However, do keep in mind that there is a trend favoring the use of web pages for tax reporting and submission of tax returns.

You can request copies of these forms from the tax entity. Some tax entities automatically mail the forms to the taxpayer. Taxpayers can print or download the forms from the tax entity's website. Other entities may be authorized to provide these forms, but the taxpayer that is ultimately responsible for acquiring and using the format approved by the taxing entity and a version that is valid.

4. SUBMIT TAX RETURNS AND REPORTS TO THE RELEVANT TAX JURISDICTIONS.

Taxpayers are required to use the format dictated by the tax authorities for the completion of their tax returns and other reporting requirements. Available options include using printed forms; using software to format the data for uploading on a tax authority's website; or using the forms available on the tax authority's website. It is up to the taxpayer to determine which method is best for him or her.

Tax authorities have made it easy for taxpayers to electronically process tax returns and reports and to upload any related data files. Websites have been configured to accept tax data. Software has been developed to help taxpayers process their data. However, some tax authorities still accept printed copies of tax returns, but only smaller and/or simpler tax returns and reports.

Taxpayers can easily find information about the options available to them on the tax authority's website. Taxpayers may also consult their tax advisers and other available resources. And, if the taxpayer finds no answer, he or she may easily call the tax authority's helpline for guidance.

5. REMIT PAYMENT FOR TAX BALANCES, OR ADDRESS ANY CREDITS.

Tax remittance refers to the monies that are due and payable to a tax authority. These remittances include calculated taxes, the accrued sales taxes that have been collected from customers, accrued use taxes, penalties, and interest.

The monies may be submitted by way of check, credit card, electronic payment system, wire transfer, or bank draft, among other methods. Some of these methods require the sharing of information with the tax authority, such as a bank account number and the bank's routing number.

If the taxpayer does not remit the monies owed in a timely manner, then he or she will likely be penalized, incur a late fee, and/or be charged interest. Some tax authorities may allow payment plans, including tax relief payment plans, if the taxpayer has some challenges with paying his or her balance in full. In some situations, penalties and interest may be waived. However, these payment plans or waived amounts must be substantiated and approved by the tax authority.

Tax authorities take certain steps to encourage and/or remind taxpayers to pay their balances. Sometimes, a tax authority will provide the taxpayer with a reminder of an overdue return in the form of a letter, email, or a notice in the taxapayer's website tax account. Some tax authorities share names and information of delinquent taxpayers on their websites as a matter of public record. If these steps do not motivate the taxpayer to pay his or her tax balances, then the taxing authority may penalize the business, which may extend to penalizing the business owners and/or other identified responsible parties. On the extreme end, the tax authority may initiate liens on assets and/or rescind any permits or licenses to do business.

Emphasis: If a taxpayer does not remit the accrued sales taxes collected from his or her customers to the appropriate tax authority, then he or she will likely incur financial penalties. In the most grievous cases, the consequences may include charges of theft or embezzlement.

6. KEEP RECORDS.

Another of the taxpayer's responsibilities is recordkeeping. Taxpayers are required to keep proof that they filed their tax returns, including any supporting documentation, along with proof of tax remittances, tax credits, and refunds as prescribed by law.

Tax returns, reports, and communications are legal documents that should be treated as such. From this perspective, businesses must retain these records and make them available to tax auditors, or any other legally authorized representative, as required by tax law.

Keeping copies of tax returns safe and readily available is a very smart business practice. Businesses use these documents to substantiate their business activities and tax compliance. They may also use them to prove compliance to their customers and/or other interested parties. Internal tax departments may audit the records in order to identify weaknesses in the business's tax procedures and/or accounting personnel. These records will most likely be used during a tax audit by an accounting firm.

SUMMARY

Tax reporting is required by taxpayers and involves submission of tax returns, tax remittance, and recordkeeping activities. Tax reporting and tax remittance provides the taxpayer with a method of measuring and comparing his or her tax responsibilities. Tax authorities will use the data to detect potential noncompliance and to monitor industrial and economic performance and trends.

In general, tax authorities share some commonalities in the steps they take and in the way they advise taxpayers to prepare for and complete their tax reporting, remittance, and recordkeeping responsibilities. As taxpayers become more familiar with these steps, it is easier for them to understand and comply with the requirements.

See Appendix 3: Tax Reporting Forms, which includes samples of forms used for tax reporting purposes.

Chapter 7

Tax Audits by Tax Authorities

Tax authorities use tax audits primarily to verify that a taxpayer is complying with tax laws. Other goals include (1) to collect any taxes due, along with any imposed fines, penalties, and/or interest; (2) identify and address tax evasion; (3) promote voluntary tax compliance; and (4) identify and inform the taxpayer of any recordkeeping issues so that the taxpayer may correct these and avoid future tax compliance issues. Altogether, the ultimate goal of a tax audit is to encourage the highest level of tax compliance by taxpayers.

GENERAL OVERVIEW OF A TAX AUDIT

Tax audits involve the interviewing of the representatives or employees of the business, acquiring an understanding of the business's practices, and the reviewing of business accounting records. Some audits may cover part of the business's activities, and others may cover all its activities related to taxes.

Some tax authorities will perform the audits either using their own employees or hiring an authorized third party. If a third party is used, keep in mind that these auditors have similar authority as the employees of the tax authority.

Tax audits may be conducted in field offices and/or remote locations. Field audits may include visits by the auditor to the auditee's business office(s) and/or other business locations. Remote audits are where the auditor works from his or her office and requests that the auditee provide him or her with relevant data and/or documents via different media, such as email, facsimile (fax), regular postal service, or common carrier.

There are several steps involved in a tax audit. The descriptions and explanations of these steps are made available for public viewing on tax authority's website as a matter of public record. Look for auditors' manuals and other publications that include descriptions of the audit steps as these may be used by the auditors as a guide and for their training.

Included in the auditors' manuals are explanations and samples of tax transactions that may help them to identify noncompliance. Use these to double-check the auditor's work and to help you understand your degree of compliance or noncompliance. Other publications and websites may contain the same information as the auditors' manuals, but with a different audience in mind: the taxpayer.

In general, the steps involved in a tax audit are as follows:

1. identifying a potential auditee
2. sending the audit notification
3. holding the initial conference with the auditee
4. receiving the auditee's authorizations
5. holding the entrance conference
6. determining the audit's scope
7. collecting and sharing data
8. determining the auditing method
9. examining the records
10. making assessments and submitting results
11. performing reconciliation
12. allowing for the contesting of audit results
13. waiving the audit assessment
14. closing the audit
15. considering the lessons learned.

Depending on the auditor, auditee, and scope, some of these steps may overlap or occur simultaneously, and some may not be needed.

Consideration: As a taxpayer, you are entitled to a copy of the tax auditor's manual, which is a public record. You should access it and become familiar with the steps before being audited.

IDENTIFYING A POTENTIAL AUDITEE

Tax authorities use different strategies for selecting potential auditees. Some use computers to analyze and identify auditees. This process is supposed to be based on random selection. Some auditees are selected based upon a specific event, a tip, or a whistleblower's report of questionable business activities or noncompliance. Some auditees are selected based on their business size, their sales volume, and/or the complexity of their tax returns. Ultimately, the selection of an auditee will depend on at least one of the established audit triggers.

The selection strategy may also involve consideration of the potential return on investment versus the cost of completing an audit. Tax authorities have determined it is usually more cost-effective and rewarding to audit larger businesses as opposed to smaller businesses. Sole proprietors have also been identified as a group who are known to prepare their own tax returns, which are more likely to contain errors. Another filtering tool is the use of preaudit questionnaires that are sent to potential auditees in order to help decide whether the responses indicate it is worthwhile to pursue an audit. It is best to answer these questionnaires truthfully and return them as required.

Another method used to identify potential auditees is analysis of an entity's sales tax returns. Most recent tax returns are compared with prior returns from a number of years in order to identify audit triggers such as (1) abnormal spikes or dips in sales revenue, (2) late returns, and (3) errors on returns. Tax returns may also be compared against those of other companies that are similar in size, that operate within the same industry, and whose activities are similar in order to identify any abnormalities.

Another way to identify auditees is by a valid lead from a whistleblower. In order to encourage whistleblowers and facilitate the submission of these reports, tax authorities offer telephone numbers and websites that the whistleblower may use to confidentially report any perceived noncompliance. However, before a tax audit is initiated, the information will be reviewed to determine its validity and whether an audit is worthwhile to pursue.

Auditors may also use findings from one audit to identify another potential auditee. It is important to understand that some auditors are authorized to share noncompliance findings with other tax authorities, which may result in that tax authority's selection of that taxpayer for a tax audit.

Basically, it has become easier for auditors to identify potential auditees and to determine which taxpayers to exclude from audits. Auditors use the different tools available to them to find auditees who are worthwhile to pursue. Tax auditors keep historical records of noncompliance, their notes, and the results of previous tax audits. They use computers to analyze and compare amounts reported on tax returns against statistics from businesses operating in similar industries. Understanding how auditees are selected may help you to prepare for an audit and/or help you to understand why you have been chosen for an audit.

SENDING THE AUDIT NOTIFICATION

Auditors are required to give notice to the auditee who has been selected for an audit, stating the intent to audit the auditee's records. Auditors must take reasonable steps to contact the auditee and provide this notice. Usually, they depend on the contact information provided by the auditee when he or she registered for a sales tax permit or a business license and/ or previously submitted tax returns.

Audit notices may also be delivered by various methods. Normally, notice is sent via a letter mailed to the business address that has been provided by the auditee. Some auditors may make the initial contact via a telephone call using the telephone number on record. If these methods fail to result in a response from the auditee, the auditor may show up at the address that has been provided. If all these methods fail to result in contact with the auditee, the auditor will surely pursue a tax assessment without any participation from the auditee.

It is wise for an auditee not to ignore any audit notice as tax audits are unavoidable. If you try to evade an audit notice or ignore an auditor, know that the tax auditor is empowered to make a tax assessment without your participation. For this, an analysis of your business will be performed, with the results used to determine and impose a tax assessment for which you, the taxpayer, will be liable. This will most likely be more costly than if you actually participated in the audit. So, your best strategy is to respond and participate as needed. You may be surprised to find that tax auditors are understanding and are willing to work with you when they can.

Emphasis: Upon receipt of a tax audit notice or questionnaire, be sure to notify the appropriate personnel within your organization and consider you audit strategy.

HOLDING THE INITIAL CONFERENCE WITH THE AUDITEE

Upon making initial contact with the taxpayer's representative, the auditor will move to collect basic information. This conference may be in the form of an in-person interview at a designated place and time, usually at the auditee's office, or may occur via a telephone call that may or may not be scheduled for a specific time.

Most tax auditors will work around the taxpayer's schedule. If the taxpayer is extremely busy, the auditor, usually flexible, will compromise. However, the auditor must adhere to certain limitations and follow specific guidance.

Now, keep in mind, it is easy for auditors to notice a taxpayer's attempt to avoid or procrastinate when they are trying to set up an initial meeting. Be aware that patterns of avoidance or procrastination may be perceived as a sign that the taxpayer is trying to hide something. So, if you have a valid reason to delay the initial contact with the auditor, be frank and honest, and do your best to comply. Usually, the auditor will be understanding and will work with you.

During the initial conversation, the auditor should explain the audit process and will ask the taxpayer's representative for some basic information about the business. The auditor may provide the auditee with some documents such as a list of the auditee's rights, a formal notice of the audit, questionnaires, and/or authorization forms. If the forms are not physically handed to the auditee, the auditor will likely either email them to the auditee or inform the auditee how to access them.

The depth of information requested by the auditor at this time will vary depending on the auditor's preparation, experience, and knowledge of the taxpayer's business. But usually basic information is discussed at this time, such as the auditee's business size, business structure, operations, and locations.

Generally, the initial conference serves to formally introduce the participants to each other and to initiate the audit and/or a preaudit review. It may also be used to identify the authorized personnel, exchange contact information, describe the initial scope of the audit, lay out the expectations for each party, and provide other information. The auditee will be allowed the opportunity to ask some questions about what to expect.

RECEIVING THE AUDITEE'S AUTHORIZATIONS

Before an auditor may proceed with his or her audit, he or she is required to identify the business's authorized representative(s) with whom he or she is to interact and from whom he or she is to collect certain data and documents. This will involve providing signed documents that may list the authorized people and their roles. Most, if not all, of the requested authorizations are required before the audit may proceed. Failure to share the information or grant any of the required authorizations may lead to unnecessary delays, problems, assessments, and/or penalties.

Some of the authorizations that are usually required include the following:

- Power of attorney. This is required when a third party is used to represent the auditee.
- Declaration of an employee to represent the auditee. With this, the auditor may confirm that he or she is working with the person who is authorized to meet with and exchange information with the auditor.
- Authorization to send and receive information and documents via email.

- Authorization for the extension of the statute of limitations. This occurs when the audit takes longer than expected, so some of the transactions go beyond the statute of limitations.
- Other authorizations as needed.

Emphasis: The authorizations forms are legal documents and should be respected as such.

HOLDING THE ENTRANCE CONFERENCE

Most auditors will conduct an entrance conference in order to gather more information to supplement that which was previously collected. This conference may take place in a formal setting or via informal communications with authorized personnel such as telephone conversations, questionnaire(s), letters, and emails. Keep in mind, the entrance conference may be combined with the initial conference meeting or may be informally conducted via conversation, email, and/ or letter.

When the entrance conference occurs, the taxpayer should be prepared to answer some in-depth questions regarding the business, including its scope of activities, its footprint, and the personnel involved.

Areas for which an auditor may be required to collect information include the following:

- Personnel—in order to understand responsible parties and the roles of relevant personnel.
- Products and services—what is sold and where.
- Industry—whether the business is a manufacturer, fabricator, wholesaler, retailer, service provider, or some other entity.
- Customers—the primary customers and what they do.
- Information systems—how the accounting data is recorded and maintained.
- Recordkeeping—how the records are kept, where they are kept, and how and when they may be reproduced.

Don't be surprised if the entrance conference is short or if it occurs over several meetings and/or conversations. All of this will depend upon factors such as the auditee's responses and their clarity. And don't be surprised if you are asked to provide documents and/or electronic data for some of these meetings.

DETERMINING THE AUDIT'S SCOPE

At or near the beginning of an audit, steps will be taken to identify the audit's scope. The auditor will share with the auditee a list of items to be reviewed, including taxes, transactions, data, documents, and accounting periods. The auditor will also determine the format for sharing data files, documents, and communications and whether an audit sampling and/or detail format will be employed. All these things should be determined at or near the start of the audit.

When developing the audit scope, the auditor may request information, data files, and/or documents in addition to those previously made available to the auditor. The auditor will review these along with all the items already collected. This review will help the auditor to acquire a clearer understanding of the business practices and effectively determine the audit scope.

Some auditors are required to complete a form to formally define the audit's objective and scope. This form will be presented to the auditee for his or her signature as a formal acknowledgment of his or her understanding of the audit scope. This document should be kept as a legal document.

The scope may also be communicated orally to the auditee; however, a letter or email should be sent to the auditee to officially document the objective and scope of the audit. Be sure to save this letter or email.

The auditee, in turn, should ask questions if the scope is not clearly defined.

The following items are usually defined and agreed upon by both parties as components of the audit scope:

Audit period. Usually, tax audits cover three or four years' worth of accounting periods. Some audits may cover either a shorter or longer period. If shorter, it may be because of a specific alert or question.

Audit method. The auditor should identify the review format, which may be a sampling or detailed, or a combination of both.

Auditee's representative. The person who represents the auditee should be sufficiently familiar with the business, the business's processes, the business's records, and the business's taxes. This person should be available and be able to promptly respond to the auditor's request for information, data, and/or documents.

Records. The auditor must have access to the records that are relevant (or copies thereof) and no more.

Requests for records usually include tax returns, financial records (such as balance sheets, general ledger records, and sales and procurement journals), and/or asset records. Keep in mind that there is no need to provide the auditor with more records than needed unless it will benefit your position. Otherwise, it may lead to delays or confusion, or expose other issues such as noncompliance.

Tax authority. Auditors should identify the tax authority and the jurisdiction that the audit covers. The auditor will not have authority to audit records for jurisdictions other than those that he or she has been formally authorized to represent.

Even though most audits adhere to the originally defined scope, the auditor may find a reason to expand the scope after the audit review process has started. Auditees may also be able to contribute feedback that may affect the auditor's decision regarding the scope. If a change is made to the scope, it may be because of several factors, such as finding hints of tax fraud, tax evasion, and/or flagrant abuse. If the original audit scope changes, the auditee should request that this be documented.

Emphasis: To avoid any problems, auditees should clearly understand the audit scope at the beginning of the audit.

COLLECTING AND SHARING DATA

Since tax auditors are authorized to examine the books and records of a tax auditee, they are authorized to request access to any and all relevant records and documents in order to achieve this goal. Auditors may also ask for some of the items to be presented in a specific format, such as a Microsoft Excel file or hardcopy. If so requested, the auditee should do his or her best to timely furnish all the items to the auditor in the format requested.

Requested items may include, but are not be limited to, the following:

- list of officers and business owners
- organizational chart
- chart of accounts
- description of the business's activities
- financial statements
- general ledgers and any subsidiary ledgers and journals
- sales and purchase journals
- customer's exemption certificates
- vendor invoices
- contracts, bids, purchase orders, work release orders, and agreements relating to the transactions
- worksheets, documents, and data that support tax returns.

As the auditee, you should provide all the requested data and documents that are relevant to the audit scope in a timely manner. However, should you find a document that may demonstrate tax compliance that the auditor did not request, feel free to offer it to him or her. If it is indeed relevant, the auditor should accept it and consider it when determining tax compliance. If the auditor finds it does not substantiate compliance, then he or she should be able to explain to you his or her reasoning for disagreeing. If he or she does not offer an explanation, ask for it as part of your learning process so you may determine whether it would be of any value when contesting the audit result.

Emphasis: There is no need to provide any document that the auditor does not request or that is outside the scope of the audit unless it will demonstrate that you were indeed tax compliant.

DETERMINING THE AUDIT METHOD

Before an auditor may start to examine transactions and determine any assessments, he or she should identify the auditing method he or she will be using. The two most common audit methods are detailed and sampling. Each method may be used for all segments of an audit or may be employed for only one segment of the audit, with the other method being used for another segment. The method selected and its application will depend upon factors such as the business, the volume of transactions, and/or the complexity of the transactions.

The **detailed audit method** involves the examination of every transaction. This method may become resource-intensive, so it is usually used for small businesses or for businesses with a relatively small number of records to examine.

The **sampling audit method**, which is more complicated than the detailed method, is based on a selection of transactions used to represent groups of transactions. This method is usually used with medium- and large-sized businesses as it is less expensive to employ than the detailed method.

When using the sampling method, many records must be examined. The transactions may be grouped into segments wherefrom some samples will be selected. Groupings may be based on dollar amounts of sales, such as sales amounts less than one thousand dollars; sales amounts greater than one thousand dollars and less than one hundred thousand dollars; and sales amounts equal to or greater than one hundred thousand dollars. The findings of the sample population will be considered to represent the entire population for that segment, and for this, an assessment will be applied to that segment of transactions. If the sampling method is selected, be sure that the selected samples are reasonably representative of the population in each group.

As the auditee, you should be able to request that one or the other method be used. But in doing so, you should consider the benefit of selecting one over the other. For some, detailed audits are preferential, especially when there is a manageable number of records and when there is reasonable confidence in the business's tax compliance, processes, and procedures. If you choose this option, be extra careful about your tax compliance.

EXAMINING THE RECORDS

The audit phase for the examination of records consists of the auditor's analysis and review of the transactions, the data, and the documents provided. This phase will formally start after the audit method has been decided on and after the data and documents have been provided to the auditor. The auditor will use available tools to facilitate the analysis of the data provided and will conduct a visual examination of documents and systems. Altogether, the auditor will strive to identify any noncompliance, applicable assessments, and/or overpayment of taxes.

The auditor's primary tool will likely be a computer. The auditee will likely be asked to present e-files in certain formats. Software may be used to analyze the e-files that are provided. This will facilitate the identification and marking of questionable transactions and the identification of those that are to be eliminated from the review. The same will be used to facilitate the calculation of any assessments or overpayments. For this, the auditor may request that the data file be in spreadsheet format and contain specific columns of data.

Following are examples of data files that may be requested, along with the required fields:

> **Procurement journal**—seller's names, addresses, order dates, item descriptions, general ledger codes, costs, and tax amounts.

Sales journal—buyer's names, addresses, invoice dates, item descriptions, general ledger codes, costs, and tax amounts.

Chart of accounts—account codes, descriptions, and account types (e.g., asset, liability, receivables).

Assets—asset identification codes, asset descriptions, acquisition dates and values, disposition dates, and depreciation methods, schedules, and values.

During the actual examination of the data and documents, the auditor will look for proof that the auditee was noncompliant or will verify the level of tax compliance. The auditor may ask some questions and/or request more data or documents in order to clarify any discrepancies or questionable activity. If this occurs, be as helpful as you can, which the auditor will appreciate. And the clarification you provide may result in a decision in your favor.

During his or her review, the auditor will likely employ the following steps:

- Review documents in order to verify their validity.
- Determine whether the appropriate tax rates were billed, the appropriate amount of taxes were paid, and whether the taxes were collected for the appropriate jurisdiction.
- Determine whether items were taxable or whether the buyer provided valid exemption certification when he or she was not billed for sales taxes on taxable items.
- Determine whether the appropriate use taxes were paid or whether the auditee took advantage of a tax exemption when his or her vendor did not bill sales taxes on taxable items.
- Determine whether accrued and remittable taxes were remitted in a timely manner to the appropriate tax authorities.
- Determine whether the appropriate tax returns and other reporting materials were completed as required.

Auditors have the authority to remove some transactions and add other transactions to the audit as long as these fit with the scope of the audit. If this occurs, you should ask the auditor to explain the basis for this action.

The auditor should not change the initially selected samples after starting the examination without a reasonable basis for doing so.

The auditor's examination of the data and documents will usually be timely. However, sometimes an auditor will need more time to complete the review. If such is the case, the auditor should communicate this to the auditee. The auditor may ask the auditee to sign a form, such as a waiver of the statute of limitations, to extend the time the auditor is allowed to complete his or her review. If the auditee refuses to agree to the extension, the auditor will likely have the option of invoking his or her ability to make his or her assessment based on the data on hand. So, strongly consider whether or not you will agree to sign such a waiver.

Emphasis: You must prove you have been compliant in terms of your tax responsibilities. In order to do this, be prepared to provide copies of invoices, purchase orders, contracts, estimates, emails, and any other documentation that may demonstrate your compliance. You may also reach out to your sellers and/or buyers and ask for documentation to support your claim of compliance.

MAKING ASSESSMENTS AND SUBMITTING RESULTS

After an auditor has completed his or her examination of the data and documents, he or she will move on to calculate any applicable assessments, nonassessments, and/or overpayments. The auditor may present an initial report to the auditee that will describe the auditor's findings and make any recommendations to waive any penalties and interest to be assessed.

After any assessment has been calculated, the auditor will present the findings to his or her supervisor for review and authorization. Once the supervisor agrees, the auditor will provide the auditee with a formal letter of assessment or nonassessment. The auditee will be allowed a reasonable amount of time to review the assessment results and to provide additional information and documentation to prove his or her compliance.

Feel free to ask questions about any assessments. Take this opportunity to understand the assessment and, if possible, find proof to verify and/or support your claim of compliance. Sometimes, you as the auditee may have to ask for more time, in which case you may have to sign a waiver of the statute of limitations.

If it has not already been done, the auditee should consider approaching the auditor with a request to consider a reduction or waiver of assessments, penalties, or interest, especially if the auditee is experiencing financial hardship. The auditor may take other circumstances into consideration when deciding whether or not to grant a reduction in the assessment, penalties, and/or interest. The auditee should check the applicable tax laws, audit manuals, and publications, and with consultants, for hints that may help to identify situations that may make this possible. Of course, if the auditor agrees, he or she will likely need to acquire authorization from his or her supervisor.

At this time, the auditor may conduct an exit conference and present the audit report. If so, he or she should take time to explain the report, its findings, and the options available to the auditee.

PERFORMING RECONCILIATION

If the auditee disagrees with the audit findings and/or assessments, he or she has two options to discuss such disagreement and try to come to some reconciliation. The first option is a reconciliation conference, and the second is an independent audit review.

A **reconciliation conference** is where the auditee can meet with the auditor and/or the auditor's supervisor to discuss any differences in findings or assessments. All parties should make a sincere attempt to resolve the differences identified by the audit. If this conference does not resolve all differences, then an independent audit review conference may be requested.

An **independent audit review conference** is where a third party will be made available to discuss and resolve any outstanding differences. The participating parties should include, at the least, the auditee, the auditor, and the auditor's supervisor. But don't be surprised if this third party is another employee of the taxing authority.

After the two conference options have been either taken advantage of or waived, a final determination will be made. The audit schedules will be finalized, reviewed by the auditor's supervisor and/or other required personnel, and then presented to the auditee to address. At this point the auditee may be able to take advantage of another option to contest the findings.

ALLOWING FOR THE CONTESTING OF AUDIT RESULTS

After an auditee has been presented with the final assessment of his or her audit and he or she is still not in agreement with it, then he or she should consider a different strategy from this point on. Basically, the auditee has two choices: (1) agree to and pay the assessment without further contesting the results or (2) contest the assessment, or part thereof, in an attempt to acquire a more favorable ruling.

Should the auditee decide to contest the assessment, he or she has a couple of options to consider, the first of which is to ask for a redetermination. If the result of the redetermination is still not agreeable to the auditee, then he or she may proceed with the second option, an audit hearing.

For the redetermination, the auditee must compose a statement of grounds to describe the dispute and the contested items. This statement must be presented to the designated tax authority in a timely manner. In fact, it should be postmarked by the deadline defined by the tax statutes or tax authority. There may be some follow-up communications, which the auditee should address as required and in a timely manner.

An audit hearing is another option to use for contesting any disputed items. This occurs through a formal hearing process. When using this mechanism, the auditee will be allowed to contest any findings and/or assessments with which he or she is still in disagreement. Note that this process may be much more time-consuming and result in extra costs.

Should an auditee want to contest an audit assessment, he or she should consider the potential or perceived benefits of the challenge as compared to the costs of the challenge. The challenge will surely cost some time and money to pursue. Also, the resulting decision may not be in the auditee's favor.

WAIVING THE AUDIT ASSESSMENT

After the audit assessment phase is completed, the formal audit assessment will be presented to the auditee. If the auditee owes any monies, these will likely include fines, penalties, and/or interest. These are the added costs an auditee should consider when deciding whether to request a waiver.

Sometimes an auditor may consider factors found during the audit and will issue a waiver without waiting for the auditee to request one. If the auditor does not offer a waiver, the auditee should consider requesting a waiver of these costs. If the auditor offers a partial waiver, the auditee should consider requesting a waiver for the remainder of the cost. It shouldn't hurt anything to try.

An auditor may consider the following factors when deciding to process a partial or full waiver:

- the knowledge level of the auditee
- whether this audit is the business's first tax audit
- any abnormal events that may affect the auditee's ability to be compliant
- whether noncompliance rates are low relative to the volume of transactions
- whether the business has demonstrated a desire to improve tax compliance
- whether the business's financial standing is weak
- the auditee's level of cooperation or resistance toward the audit.

Some auditors may require that the auditee formally request any waiver by using a letter, form, and/or email. This request should include the reason(s) for requesting the waiver and for which aspect of the assessment. When applicable, the auditee should include a reminder that there he or she sincerely cooperated with the auditor.

Emphasis: It does not hurt to ask for a reduction or the waiver of part or all of the fines, penalties, or interest. The worst that can happen is that your request will be denied.

CLOSING THE AUDIT

After the auditee is presented with the final notice of assessment and he or she agrees with this, the auditor will attend to several matters, as follows:

1. Final letter of assessment

At the close of the audit, the auditor should present a formal assessment letter to the auditee. This letter should describe the audit, its findings, and assessments or refunds. Be sure to keep this letter.

Auditees may find that the assessment letter and other communications may be needed for future audit-related inquiries. There may come a time when the auditee will need to present these documents to other tax auditors whose inquiries may overlap with this audit. Such communications may also be used to substantiate that you have been previously audited on the specific transactions or range of transactions. In effect, the assessment letter may save you some money.

2. Settlement

If the auditee owes an assessment, then he or she should be sure to follow the auditor's instructions for the payment thereof. If the auditee requires a payment schedule, then he or she should ask the auditor for such. If afterward the auditee finds that he or she is unable to comply with the agreed payment schedule, he or she should notify the auditor or other appropriate person and explain his or her situation. If needed, the auditee should request a revised payment schedule.

3. **Audit review or survey**

Another step of the audit closure phase is a review of the auditor, which is basically a survey of the auditor and his or her performance. This is authorized by the taxing authority and is usually presented in questionnaire form. Some audit reviews may be verbal. Generally, the purpose of this review is to collect feedback related to the audit and to evaluate the auditor's performance so he or she may improve on his or her audit process.

With the audit review, the auditee will be able to grade the audit and the auditor's performance. Some of the questions may be generic, and answers may be in a multiple choice and/or true/false questionnaire format. Most reviews allow the auditee an opportunity to make additional comments and share suggestions. Take advantage of this opportunity as, at your next audit, you may benefit from any improvements implemented based on the results of the review.

Emphasis: An audit review or survey should not be used to share angry or hateful thoughts, as this will not be helpful. It should be completed as objectively and professionally as possible.

4. **Documents and communications**

Lastly, be sure to save any communications related to the audit. If possible, keep the files that were presented to the auditor, especially those that are not easily reproducible. These may come handy if you are audited again as they will help you save time. By keeping this information, you will be able to declare whether a selected item was previously audited and, if applicable, taxes were assessed and paid.

Sometimes, your vendors and/or customers will reach out to you when they are undergoing an audit. The documents you saved may come in handy when you are asked to provide proof of compliance. They may demonstrate to the auditor that you were in compliance or have addressed any instances of noncompliance.

Another consideration is that some transactions may be audited by more than one tax jurisdiction. This occurs when two tax authorities have jurisdiction over the same transaction, for example, a sold item is shipped from one state to another for delivery to the customer. With these documents in hand, you may easily clarify facts and/or answer any questions.

Emphasis: Keep all records of communications. These may be needed for future audits or when you are requested by vendors, customers, and/or their tax auditors to provide proof of compliance.

CONSIDERING THE LESSONS LEARNED

Some businesses will use the findings from their tax audits to proactively analyze and improve their business practices with a goal of improving their tax compliance. This process involves considering the auditor's observations and findings, analyzing the business for any weaknesses, and determining what will be required to improve on these weaknesses.

Items to be considered may include the following:

- Were the appropriate taxes billed to taxable customers? If not, why not?
- Were the appropriate taxes on taxable transactions paid to vendors?
- What software and/or equipment is needed to identify taxable versus nontaxable items, tax rates, tax jurisdictions, etc.?
- Do the employees need training?
- Do any of the auditor's suggestions or findings require further action?
- Did the auditor find all incidents of noncompliance?

SUMMARY

The goals of a tax audit include the identification of any noncompliance, identification of any taxes owed, and collection of taxes, fines, and fees, all while making an effort to minimize the costs of the audit. Other goals include the identification of deliberate noncompliance and the sharing with the auditee any of his or her business practices that may contribute to noncompliance. To achieve these goals, auditors will review an auditee's business records, documents, and procedures, along with making inquiries with other businesses and people.

At the start of an audit, an auditor will review the business's records and documents with multiple purposes in mind, one of which is to identify the scope of the audit. Another purpose is to identify the specific transactions to be audited. The auditor does this review as part of his or her actual review and analysis for tax compliance and assessment determination.

In general, the auditee is deemed responsible for providing proof of compliance with any applicable tax laws, such as evidence that the applicable taxes were indeed paid for taxable transactions or that the appropriate exemption certificate was collected from customers. Proof is needed to substantiate that the taxes collected from customers were either remitted to the appropriate taxing authority or returned when needed. Generally, almost all the proof that must be given to the auditor will be in the form of a record, document, or email.

If an auditee is found to be noncompliant by an audit, then he or she may have to pay the taxes owed along with fines, penalties, and interest, and/ or have his or her authority to do business in the jurisdiction withdrawn. However, if the noncompliant activities are found to be flagrant and deliberate, the auditee may face jail time. Along with cost considerations, these consequences are strong reasons to be as compliant as possible with tax laws and tax responsibilities.

Chapter 8

Management of Transactional Taxes

Most businesses set up formal policies and procedures to manage each of their department's activities and business strategies. Some businesses completely forget to include considerations for transactional taxes. In doing so, these businesses expose themselves to avoidable costs and understated costs. Smaller businesses or those just starting are less likely to establish a separate formal tax department because of resource limitations. Other businesses may instantly recognize the benefits of formalizing their tax management processes. Regardless of whether it is done formally or informally, addressing transactional taxes as an everyday business practice is imperative.

Various factors affect the size of the staff of a tax department, such as the organization's budget and the availability of qualified candidates. Smaller businesses usually budget less money for this than larger businesses do. Smaller businesses are more apt to depend on their staffs to take on more than one department's responsibilities and roles. So, a dedicated tax department is less likely to exist in a small business. On the other hand, larger businesses usually can afford the cost of establishing and maintaining a tax department and staffing it with experienced personnel. This department may be composed of one or more persons. Larger businesses are also more apt to take advantage of tax-related tools such as tax consultants, tax-related software, and/or services that may affect the size of the tax department.

Regardless of its size, a business should consider the benefits of acquiring and using any available tools that may help to maximize their compliance with tax laws and minimize their tax costs. These tools may save the tax personnel time in research and quickly provide accurate up-to-date information. Basically, these tools may turn out to be an investment for the business, and as such, they may save thousands of dollars in research, resources, staff salaries, and/or audit assessments.

Emphasis: Do not let a tax audit be your motivator. Instead, be proactive and develop your tax strategies, policies, processes, and staff as soon as your business is started up. Modify these strategies as your business grows or as needed.

BUSINESS GROUPS IMPACTED BY TRANSACTIONAL TAXES

Businesses should always consider the scope and impact of transactional taxes on their business strategies. Things such as budgets, activities, processes, and procedures need to be analyzed, established, and implemented in order to effectively manage the taxes. Qualified personnel should be employed to manage any applicable taxes.

Transactional taxes directly impact many of a business's groups and indirectly impact the remaining business groups. It is important to recognize how every business group is affected.

Following are groups of business activities that are usually directly affected by transactional taxes:

Business management	• Business registration
	• Tax-related registrations (permits, licenses, etc.)
	• Accounting information systems
Operations	• Estimating
	• Procurement
	• Sales
	• Customer billing
	• Accounts receivable
	• Accounts payable
Tax compliance	• Tax reporting
	• Tax audits (internal and external)
	• Training

When a business group is directly impacted by transactional taxes, this impact should be consciously considered, especially when it concerns the development of the business's budget, processes, and procedures. Taxes will need to be allocated and paid. Processes and procedures will need to be developed to manage the taxes.

Each affected business group should understand the impact of taxes on its activities. Taxes will be paid on purchases. Customers are to be billed taxes and/or must present exemption certificates. Collected taxes and/or use taxes need to be reported and remitted. Trained personnel are needed to perform these actions.

DIRECT IMPACT OF TRANSACTIONAL TAXES

Following is a brief description of each of the previously identified departments or business groups and a mention of how they are directly impacted by taxes. Businesses should consider these descriptions in order to understand and address the responsibilities imposed upon taxpayers by taxing authorities.

Business Management

Business registration. Businesses need to determine whether they need to register with any tax authority in order to establish their business and/or do business in the relevant tax jurisdiction. The business may be registered as a partnership, sole proprietorship, corporation, or foreign corporation.

Tax-related registrations (permits, licenses, etc.). Depending on the business activities and nexus, a business may have to apply for permits, licenses, and any other authorizations in order to conduct business in certain tax jurisdictions. The business may also be required to register for exemptions and tax discounts. Such permits may include sales tax permits, business licenses, and exemption certificates.

Accounting information systems. Each business should use an accounting recordkeeping system that enables the business to easily track and manage its transactional taxes. The system needs to be configured to facilitate tax tracking, tax calculation, transaction history monitoring, and report generation. This may be as simple as setting up general ledger codes and vendor accounts for remittances to tax authorities. It may also involve the identification and setup of codes for tax jurisdictions and rates. A more sophisticated system will be configured in such a way that users may be able to identify what products or services are taxable when sold. There are many third-party companies that provide consulting services, software, and/or information to advise and/or supplement a business's accounting system. The recordkeeping system should be able to generate reports to provide information that will facilitate the processing of tax reports and tax returns, and the identification of payable taxes, taxes due, etc.

Operations

Estimating. Estimating departments should consider when and how tax costs will apply to a bid or to their cost determinations. Estimates or bids should specifically indicate whether applicable taxes are included in the quoted price or whether these are listed separately as estimated tax costs.

When possible, estimators should share that the bid or estimate is potentially taxable or nontaxable.

Sales. Sales makers and order takers should know whether their sales orders are taxable. For taxable sales, they need to be prepared to request exemption certificates from their customers or inform the customer that he or she will be billed for the appropriate taxes.

Since customers are likely to ask about the dollar amount of the applicable taxes, the order takers should be prepared to provide such information or refer the customer to someone who may be able to answer these questions.

Customer billing. When billing customers, applicable taxes need to be billed for the appropriate tax jurisdiction(s) and at the appropriate rate. For this, accounting systems should include the use of general ledger accounts to track and manage the accrued taxes billed to and collected from the customers. It is important to understand that these taxes are not earnings or revenue for the business. Instead they are accruals, and they need to be remitted to the appropriate tax authorities.

The general ledger accounts used to track accrued sales taxes are usually labeled "Accrued Sales Taxes" or something similar. These accounts are normally set up as liability accounts that should be relieved when remittances are made to the appropriate tax authority.

Accounts receivable. When processing a payment that has been received from a customer, the amount received that is for the taxes billed should be posted to the general ledger account that has been designated for the accrual of these taxes. If the customer does not pay the taxes he or she has been billed, then you should either request and collect an exemption certificate or work with the customer to resolve this nonpayment.

Since a seller is usually considered the agent of the tax authority, it is the seller who will be held responsible for the billing, collection, and remittal of the taxes to the appropriate tax authority. Should a buyer refuse to pay the taxes billed and refuse to provide an exemption certificate, the seller will likely have a collections issue to resolve with the buyer.

Procurement. When buyers request quotes or bids, they should consider whether taxes are applicable. The buyer should ask vendors to (1) identify the applicable sales taxes; (2) specifically identify whether the taxes are included in the price; and/or (3) separately list all taxes on the quote or bid.

When placing a purchase order with a seller for which an exemption may be declared, the buyer must present the appropriate documentation for the declaration of the exemption.

Purchase requisitions and purchase orders should be coded as either taxable or nontaxable in the accounting information system. When possible, this should occur at the line-item level.

Accounts payable. Each vendor invoice issued should be reviewed to ensure that it is compliant in terms of tax responsibilities. When the purchase is of a nontaxable item, there is no need to be concerned about taxes.

When processing an invoice from a seller, check for the following:

- Whether taxes are applicable to the items procured.
- When tax is applicable, that the appropriate tax amount is billed and that it is for the appropriate jurisdiction(s).
- Whether an exemption may be used.
  o If an exemption is applicable, an exemption certificate should be issued to the seller in a timely manner, and the seller must ensure that he or she does not bill for the sales tax.
  o If an exemption is not applicable, the seller should bill the buyer for the sales taxes.
- When the seller refuses to, or cannot, bill for the applicable sales tax, the buyer should remit use taxes to the appropriate tax authority.
- The sales/use taxes should be appropriately coded and posted to the appropriate general ledger accounts in order to separate the taxes from the costs of the goods and/or services.

Tax Compliance

Tax reporting. The appropriate tax returns and reports will need to be processed as required by the tax authorities. For this, the information to be reported will need to be calculated—or reports from the business's accounting systems should be used. Someone will have to know what returns are to be completed and when. A person authorized to represent the business will have to review and sign the returns on behalf of the business.

Tax audits (internal and external). There are two types of tax audits, external and internal, to identify noncompliance. These audits can also be used to identify ways to improve the business's policies and procedures.

For this, a qualified person should be designated to address and manage the tax audit. This person should be familiar with taxes and should know how to gather information and documents as required.

External tax audit. An external tax audit will be performed by a tax authority, and the business will have to designate an authorized person to represent the business and work with the tax auditor.

Internal tax audit. The business should designate someone to audit the business's own books to ensure the accounting and compliance is in order. This may be a third party or an employee of the business. Either way, this person should be sufficiently knowledgeable and experienced in analyzing the books to find any instances of noncompliance and/or inefficiency, and should report such to management. Of course, compliment compliance.

Training. Each person involved with the processing of taxes should be appropriately trained to do his or her job properly. This can be as simple as understanding tax rates and how taxes are to be applied to orders, or it can be as complicated as analyzing tax laws and understanding their applicability to and impact on the business's activities and profits. Overall, management should consider each departmental process and the knowledge level of the employees involved.

Management should also consider providing useful tools to the staff, including any training in their use. When needed, training should be designed to expand the employee's knowledge of taxes for the task(s) at hand.

Some employees' knowledge level may be enhanced with simple training that includes explanations and step-by-step instructions for the tasks they are expected to complete. The depth of such training may depend on the sophistication of the accounting system.

On-the-job training will likely be customized to fit the needs of the business. It might include training in the use of any available tools, software, books, and research resources. It may involve a senior tax employee to train and mentor the less experienced employee and/or may require the employee to study on company time.

For those employees who need a higher level of knowledge of taxes, the training curriculum may involve research, self-study, third-party training courses, and the use of consultants. How this is accomplished will depend on the policies and procedures of the business and available resources.

ESTABLISHING A TAX POLICY AND PROCEDURES

Another part of a well-developed strategy for sound tax management is a formal identification of tax-related policies and procedures for the different business activities and departments. Each policy and procedure should be shared and explained; otherwise, it will be of little value. Also, it would be wasteful if the employees failed to understand the policies, their scope, and/or their purpose.

Keep in mind that policies are intended to support the business's strategies, whereas procedures define the steps one must take to complete the task.

Following is an example of how policies may be grouped and described simply:

Tax policy. Be tax compliant and minimize tax-related costs.

Tax procedures. Share relevant tax information and responsibilities with internal departments and trading partners. Keeping good records is imperative. Maximize the benefits of available exemptions and/or tax discounts.

Tax tools. Identify and procure tax tools that are relevant to the business and that may help to minimize tax costs. Develop and refine the tools as needed.

Tax staff. Personnel should have sufficient knowledge of taxes and be willing to maintain and expand their knowledge level, as well as stay informed of the latest changes in tax laws and practices.

Every business should strongly consider the value of understanding, developing, and implementing its own formal policies and procedures.

Tax Policy

Every business should establish and adhere to its own tax policy. If your tax policy reads as listed in the prior section, "To be tax compliant and minimize tax-related costs," then it is minimally ambiguous or entirely unambiguous. Indeed, it is brief and concise. Such a statement infers that your business intends to follow the tax laws and, at the same time, strives to reduce its tax costs. But this is not as simple as it sounds.

To follow this tax policy, one must gather, understand, and share a good deal of information. Also required is constant learning and research. When necessary, any impacts resulting from changes in applicable tax laws and practices should be analyzed in a timely matter and communicated. And, when needed, the policy should be modified in a timely manner.

The tax policy should be used as a reminder that tax laws are to be adhered to and that all the business's departments should be respectful of this. It should also be used to support the procedures in place.

Tax Procedures

Tax procedures span and affect various departments and tasks. As described previously, these procedures include business registration, estimates, sales, billing, procurement, accounts payable, and tax reporting. Each of these business sectors is responsible for the segment of the tax procedure that is relevant to its activities. For this, procedures related to taxes should be embedded in the procedures for carrying out the affected departmental tasks. Communication and cooperation between the different departments is crucial.

The person responsible for authorizing tax-related procedures must always be cognizant of the procedures in place and of any information that may affect these. This person should analyze changes in business activities and/or procedures, make adjustments as needed, analyze changes to tax laws and policies, and determine how these will affect the procedures already in place.

The managers of each department should understand and respect the tax-related procedures. Any questions should be directed to the appropriate personnel. Any observations and/or suggestions should be shared in order to improve the tax procedures.

Tax procedures should be modified as needed, which should be done in a timely manner. Factors that may lead to such modifications include changes in tax laws, nexus, business activities, accounting information systems, and staff. Other factors that may affect procedures are organizational changes, personnel changes, and changes in tax tools and resources. When any of these changes occur, the business should review its tax procedures in order to determine where modifications are needed.

Tax Tools

A good tax strategy will include the use of tools for the management of transactional taxes, such as software, computers, the internet, and subscriptions to tax research tools. Depending upon the need of the business and the expertise of its staff, the strategy may be as simple as using only one of these tax tools. However, in general, the larger and more complex businesses will tend to use a combination of these tools.

Each business needs to do some self-analysis in order to decide what tools to consider, acquire, and employ. Such an analysis will involve an understanding of the business's tax footprint, activities, and internal processes, and the level of its staff's skill and knowledge base. Also to be considered is affordability and the ultimate goal. Some businesses use tax consultants to perform this analysis.

After understanding all the different components involved, the business should develop a strategy for shopping for the needed tools. An analysis of the benefits and drawbacks of the different tools should be performed. Considerations include the complexity of the setup and the cost to manage the tool. Be prepared to invest some time if you wish to complete this in the appropriate manner.

Once you decide which tax tool(s) to use, review the affected procedures and modify them as needed in order to take advantage of the tool's benefits. This will require some level of analysis, authorization, and implementation, along with some level of training or information sharing. Sellers of some software will provide training sessions, staff, and/or tools for training purposes.

A successful and efficient tax compliance strategy will include the use of tax tools that complement the tax staff and the business's tax goals. For further insight on this topic, see the chapter on tax compliance goals.

Tax Staff

To successfully adhere to its tax policy, a business will need three categories of staff who will respect its tax policies and procedures: (1) managers, (2) procedure designers, and (3) workers. The management personnel will be responsible for making tax-related decisions and authorizations. Procedure designers will design, write, and implement tax procedures. And the workers will actually complete the tasks while adhering to the tax procedures and using any tax tools provided. Each individual will have to do his or her part as a member of the tax compliance team. For some businesses, one person may take on more than one of these staffing roles.

When a business does not have a good complement of staff members available, it may reach out to a third party to compensate for the personnel shortage or the weaknesses of the business's own personnel. Third-party companies will have staff members who can fill the positions that the business cannot fill with its own internal staff. If a third party is used, the individually should be sufficiently trained in taxes or have sufficient knowledge and experience to do the work that is expected of him or her.

In general, tax positions or job titles will include the following:

- tax accountant
- tax analyst
- internal tax auditor
- tax compliance analyst
- tax teacher or trainer
- tax writers
- tax auditor
- tax lawyer
- tax professional
- tax expert
- tax consultant.

Regardless of where the staff member comes from, he or she should be qualified, with the appropriate level of education, training, and/or experience to perform the tasks he or she is expected to perform. The skill set/expertise level needed from the tax staff depends upon the complexity of the tax laws associated with the business and the business's structure, policies, and procedures. Managers should be able to objectively identify whether an aptly qualified person holds the most appropriate position and when to make staff changes.

Managers should also know when any one of these tasks should be carried out:

1) training;

2) replacement of underqualified staff members;

3) hiring of qualified personnel;

4) making a change to the procedures to accommodate the weaknesses of staff members; and/or

5) acquisition of tools to enhance productivity.

SUMMARY

Every business should keep in mind that transactional taxes will make an impact on every aspect of its business strategy. A direct impact will be felt by the departments that deal directly with costs and cost tracking. An indirect impact will be felt by any supporting departments and by any departments that are directly involved with manufacturing, product development, and/or service.

Each business should do the following:

- Place some emphasis on addressing taxes and budgeting for the associated costs.
- Ensure that the required qualified resources are employed.
- Develop and adopt policies and procedures that efficiently and appropriately address taxes and tax goals.
- Manage documentation and archives as required by law.

Every business must pay its transactional taxes as required by law. Associated activities include paying or collecting taxes imposed upon transactions (procurement and sales). Some jurisdictions require the payment of taxes on revenue earned from sales. And each business must perform administrative actions such as tax reporting, tax compliance, tax audits, and the training of employees to manage this area of concern.

Overall, smart business managers will establish policies and procedures to address transactional taxes. They will identify how and where transactional taxes will affect the business's plans, budget, and contingency budget.

See Appendix 2: Application Forms for Tax Exemption, which includes samples of different application forms.

Chapter 9

Other Tax-Related Considerations

Business managers have many things to consider in terms of managing a business. One thing they must consider is the business's tax-related activities while striving for maximum tax compliance. A key strategy here is to establish a tax department that is staffed with personnel who have tax-related experience and knowledge. However, smaller businesses may not have the luxury of setting up a formal tax department, and yet, they have some of the same considerations and concerns.

As is the case with most departments, there are multiple considerations when managing a tax department or tax-related activities, including costs, qualified employees, and provision of tax tools and resources. Along with this is the implementation of appropriate policies and procedures. Good coordination of these will surely lead to a successful tax department and enhanced tax compliance.

All that aside, costs are inevitable. The amount of these costs will depend on the business's policies, procedures, and strategies. Of course, as with any of the other business departments, there is always the possibility of incurring avoidable costs. A good tax manager should be able to minimize costs by properly managing the different components and, in the meantime, maximize tax compliance.

Most of the costs related to taxes are very similar to the costs incurred by other business processes or activities. From this perspective, the tax-related costs can be treated similarly to the costs of other departments and may include the following:

- employee-related costs
- external resources
- tax tools
- tax departments
- tax policies and procedures
- archival of tax records
- contractual and other legal considerations
- civil and criminal litigation.

Managers should always be mindful of the possibility of incurring avoidable and unnecessary costs. Just as important, they should always be proactive in minimizing or eliminating these costs where possible.

Some avoidable tax-related costs may be a result of the following:

- ill-prepared or ill-trained personnel, or using unskilled personnel
- tax audits, including penalties and interests
- ineffective policies and procedures
- nonadherence to well-made policies and procedures
- failure to take advantage of external tax resources when needed
- poorly configured accounting information systems
- contractual and other legal implications.

Other tax costs that are not so easy to identify or prepare for are the unexpected costs. The possibility of incurring these costs is real. These costs may arise from tax audit assessments or from an unexpected need to hire an external tax resource and/or replace tax tools. These costs should not be ignored and should be considered when the business is developing its budget and strategy.

EMPLOYEE-RELATED COSTS

Each business should employ people who are familiar with transactional taxes and are able to address the tax-related responsibilities. The number of employees dedicated to this task will vary with the size, structure, and needs of the company. Of course, with the employment of these employees comes administrative-related costs.

In general, costs associated with employing tax employees are similar to costs associated with any other employee. Included in these costs are the following categories:

- employing qualified employees
- paying wages, salaries, and benefits
- providing continuing education and training.

The costs associated with each of these categories are affected by the employee's skill and experience and by the business's desire to retain qualified employees.

EMPLOYING QUALIFIED EMPLOYEES

As mentioned before, employing qualified tax employees is essential if a business is to successfully manage its tax compliance strategy. Having a qualified tax staff will ensure that the work is being addressed appropriately. It will also help to ensure that tax policies and procedures are adhered to.

Hiring a qualified employee usually costs more in salary than hiring a nonqualified employee. However, savings may be realized by the minimization of costs for training and the avoidance of errors.

Hiring an unqualified or ill-prepared employee may cost the business more than the savings it may be trying to achieve. The employee is likely to make costly errors such as making bad tax decisions, misinterpreting tax laws and rulings, and/or improperly completing tax returns and reports. These employees usually require some training and some time to develop.

If the business intends to keep and develop an underqualified employee, then it will likely incur costs for training and education-related activities. The employee will have to be paid for the man-hours spent to complete the training, as well as for education and other activities related to his or her development. Trainers and mentors will have to devote time to doing the training and overseeing the quality of work.

However, there are some benefits to be derived from developing such an employee. He or she will become more informed, will be more productive, and will make fewer errors, which will lessen the need for outside resources, consultants, and such.

WAGES, SALARIES, AND BENEFITS

The wages and salaries paid to tax employees should be competitive in terms of the market. Most businesses will take into consideration the job duties, level of experience, and knowledge of the employee when determining the appropriate compensation. That said, pay scales and benefits offered to employees will vary according to the business.

When an employee is paid less than the competitive market rate of compensation for a person in his or her position, the employer risks losing the employee to a business that is willing to pay him or her the market rate. Almost all employees expect to be paid appropriately and, at some time, will likely make inquiries to determine the competitive market rate. Inevitably, some employees will decide to change jobs in order to achieve a higher level of compensation.

If an employer does not offer competitive compensation, then he or she will also risk morale-related costs such as unhappy employees, slower productivity, or an increase in errors. To avoid these costs, the employer should reasonably compensate its employees for the value they bring to the business.

Many businesses are aware of morale-related issues and may give periodic raises and/or bonuses to their employees. Some bonuses serve as rewards for certain achievements, such as achieving a sales goal, and some are designed to share the profits of the business. However, I have yet to see a bonus given based on tax savings or the minimization of tax costs.

Consideration: Keeping employees' compensation at a competitive level will lead to more productive, happier, and more loyal employees.

CONTINUING EDUCATION AND TRAINING

Since tax laws and rules change periodically, employers should allocate money in their budgets for the continuing education and training of tax employees. Some of these costs may vary depending on the knowledge needed, available trainers, and access to training. Continuing education programs are designed to keep employees abreast of changing laws and the application of these laws. Providing education and training will help to reinforce and/or expand the employee's knowledge base and, at the same time, benefit the business.

Tax-related educational programs are offered in formats that may vary by provider and subject matter. Some programs are made available in the form of seminars, podcasts, handouts, and/or online education. Most of the training programs offer handouts and opportunities for the attendees to ask questions and share experiences during the sessions. The providers compete for business by offering trainees a variety of training materials and formats for use.

Some training providers offer free training. Included among these providers are tax authorities, tax professionals, and schools. The corresponding programs are usually very generic and short. Also, some programs may present repetitive information and/or information that the employee may not be familiar with. But overall, most are well worth taking advantage of, especially for employees who need introductory information and/or reinforcement to their knowledge of tax laws and the application of those laws.

The educational programs offered by tax professionals and schools may include classes that are more specific regarding specific tax laws and/or business activities. The duration of these classes may be for a few hours or a series of sessions. The costs can be as little as fifty-nine dollars and as much as one thousand dollars, or sometimes more. But before spending money on a costly program, the business manager should take time to understand the employee's knowledge base and the need to expand it, and how the program will complement the needs of the business.

Another benefit of these programs is that some providers offer continuing education units (CEU) and/or continuing education credits (CEC), which are earned by professionals such as certified public accountants (CPAs) and tax preparers to maintain professional licenses and/or certifications.

Most training providers try to offer their programs when it is most convenient for the intended audience. However, sometimes an employee may have to travel to attend a seminar or class. In most cases, the employer will pay travel-related costs in addition to the program cost.

EXTERNAL RESOURCES

When internal resources are inadequate to appropriately address tax compliance, one option to consider is external resources, which come in the form of tax consultants, tax lawyers, and professional tax services. Of course, each of these options may offer different services and products and may have different costs. Before employing an external tax resource, a business should determine whether using one is worth the cost, then determine which type of professional to hire and how long to employ that person.

Following are some considerations when deciding to employ external resources:

- employees' strengths and weaknesses
- budget considerations and management authorizations
- value of educating and/or training present employees, along with the costs and time to complete this
- replacing present employees with better- or lesser-qualified employees
- supplementing the knowledge of present employees
- any tax tools that may be beneficial
- replacing, removing, and/or enhancing the present tax tools
- how much time or how many man-hours will be required to interview and select the external resource
- how much time it will take to explain the business process and procedures to external resources, and how much time will be needed to give these resources access to internal documents and data.

Costs for external resources will vary based upon each business's strategy and on the rate to be charged. Sometimes, hiring an external resource is well worth the cost, especially if management has no confidence in the qualifications and/or decision-making of their employees. Other times, hiring an external resource may be too costly if the results are not as expected. Therefore, before employing external resources, the manager should take the time to understand what is needed and for what duration.

Tax Consultants

Tax consultants, also referred to as tax advisers or tax experts, should have the appropriate level of training and experience to provide the quality service expected of them. Consultants should conduct themselves in a professional manner, be readily available to answer tax questions, and assist as needed. They should also be willing to explain their processes, strategies, and costs, and share relevant suggestions and information with the business manager(s).

Typical services provided by a tax consultant may include one or a combination of the following:

- Analyze and/or prepare accounting reports, tax reports, tax returns, etc.
- Analyze the business's financial and legal position in order to determine tax exposure and suggest tax strategies.
- Assist with developing a business's tax policy and/or its procedures.
- Assist with, manage, and/or complete internal tax audits.
- Assist with and/or manage external tax audits.
- Configure and/or maintain tax-related software.

The cost to employ the services of a tax consultant may not be limited to labor hours. Other costs that need to be considered include deliverables, or the completion of the tasks that are requested of the consultant. Consultants may charge different fees.

Tax consultants may specialize in one or more types of tax. Because of this, the business manager should take time to ask questions in order to acquire a clear understanding of the consultant's specialty, experience, certifications, and accreditations. The answers and responses may help the manager to determine whether the consultant is right for the job, has the appropriate qualifications for the intended tasks, etc.

An easy way to verify a consultant's qualifications is to ask about earned professional certifications and/or accreditations. This is also usually a reliable method for identifying the consultant's level of tax knowledge and skills. However, keep in mind that higher qualifications will enable the consultant to charge a higher fee for his or her services and deliverables.

Some of the tax certifications and accreditations issued by professional tax organizations, governmental authorities, and/or accredited educational institutions include the following:

- certified professional accountant (CPA)
- transactional tax analyst
- a degree in accounting or taxation from an accredited university.

Other tax-related certifications and accreditations are issued for specialized tax areas. Business managers should be aware that even though the consultant has earned one or more of these certifications, he or she is not automatically qualified as an expert on transactional taxes. With this in mind, consideration should be given as to whether the consultant may have sufficient experience with transactional taxes through which he or she may have acquired the level of knowledge required to address these taxes.

Other available tax certifications and accreditations are as follows:

- accredited tax adviser (ATA)
- accredited tax consultant (ATA)
- certified payroll professional (CPP)
- certified international tax analyst
- fund tax analyst
- IRS-enrolled agent
- payroll tax analyst
- property tax analyst.

Professional Tax Service Providers

Professional tax service providers offer a variety of tax-related services such as bookkeeping, tax consulting, tax planning, and tax reporting. These providers may be an individual or a firm with sufficient qualifications and experience to adequately provide their services and deliverables. And, as with tax consultants, they can provide services for different tax types and different taxpayers.

Some professional tax service providers may only provide bookkeeping and accounting services for the different taxes. Some may be required to use their own computer systems. Some will accept data files and use these to produce the deliverables. And some may take summary accounting data or reports and process these as needed for accounting-related services.

Some tax service providers may also allow the use of their own tax software to produce deliverable tax reports, tax returns, and research information. Here, the providers may load data or results from the client's computer system or allow the client to log into the provider's website or network to access the information and software.

The providers may also offer advice on internal policies and procedures, provide answers to tax questions, and/or educate or train employees.

Some tax service providers offer tax representation for the taxpayer when dealing with the tax authorities during tax audits or other legal actions. For this, they will need to be given some level of power of attorney.

As when hiring any consultant, the business manager should weigh the costs of the different service providers against the benefits they may provide. The business manager should complete similar steps as those taken when hiring a consultant, including making similar inquiries. In most cases, professional tax service providers will be more costly and will have more limited access than an internal staff and/or tax expert. Do your research in order to make this choice.

Government-Provided Tax Assistance

Many tax authorities maintain staffs that are available to help taxpayers with tax-related questions. Some of these staff members may only be available to answer simple tax questions or direct the inquirer to a staff member who specializes in the tax matter under discussion. Others may be dedicated to answering complex tax questions and assist with the analysis of the tax situation described. Then there are some who are authorized to answer tax questions with official letter opinions or guidance.

The quantity, quality, and expertise of the assistance will vary with how the tax staff is organized and how they make themselves available to assist taxpayers. The assistants' skills will vary with experience, training, and education. Be aware, some assistants are trainees who have minimum experience and are learning about taxes as they are gaining the experience. Some are at the intermediate level with some experience and knowledge, but are still learning. Others may be considered experts in certain the tax fields or industries. Always be aware of the qualifications of the person assisting you.

When requesting assistance from the government, keep the following in mind:

- **Whether all relevant facts have been shared with the tax assistant.**

  Prior to calling for tax assistance, prepare yourself by trying to identify and have ready relevant information. During the call, the assistant may ask for information that you have not provided or may request that you clarify the information you have provided. Try to share what is relevant to your inquiry in a clear and concise manner.

- **The tax assistant's level of experience and knowledge.**

  During the conversation, listen for any clues that will help you detect the experience level of the tax assistant, including hesitation, requests for information unrelated to your inquiry, and/or sharing information that is irrelevant to your inquiry.

- **The tax assistant may not understand all the facts of the situation.**

  Make an effort to verify that the tax assistant understands any information you provide. You may ask questions to verify what the tax assistant heard from you and how he or she interpreted it. Or look for clues that there is a misunderstanding.

- **The inquirer (taxpayer) may give information that does not apply to the tax situation in question.**

    Use your logic to determine whether the information provided to you applies to your inquiry. If it does not make sense or is confusing, ask more questions to clarify.

- **The inquirer (taxpayer) is responsible for actions taken even if these are based on answers or responses provided by the tax assistant. That is, the tax assistant has no liability.**

    In general, it is the taxpayer's responsibility to decide what actions are to be taken. The tax assistant will not be held responsible for what you do unless you have documentation of his or her directives. To get a documented response to your inquiry, you can either email your inquiry or ask for a letter ruling.

- **Tax auditors will not accept verbally provided guidance from a tax assistant as an excuse for tax noncompliance unless the conversation is documented.**

    It is important to know that tax auditors will reject any verbal responses given to your inquiries. The responses will have to be documented.

Tip: Information provided by a government-based tax assistant is intended to help taxpayers understand their tax responsibilities and is not intended to override any tax responsibilities. Taxpayers will not be forgiven for following bad guidance given by any tax assistant unless it is documented.

TAX TOOLS

Tax tools may be procured and employed to increase employees' productivity and accuracy. Among the different types of tax tools available, the most predominantly used are accounting software programs that include tax modules and tax tables. The internet, tax publications, and specialized tax software programs may be used to access tax information.

To access and use some of these tax tools, users may have to pay a onetime fee, pay for a subscription, or pay for a license. Sometimes one must pay an annual fee to gain access. As with anything, the more advanced the tool, the more it costs to acquire it and use it. For this, each business manager should do some research and analysis to determine what tools are needed, which will be easy to integrate into the business's accounting systems, and whether it will be cost-effective.

The tools needed for taxes will depend on the size and needs of the business. A very small business may be able to depend upon a manual method of maintaining accounting records and complying with all its tax responsibilities. However, larger businesses will find it most beneficial to use computers and software as essential tools for bookkeeping, tax analysis, and tax reporting.

Using some of these tools will likely require some training. However, most business managers will derive some benefits from employing the different tax tools.

Computer and Software

Today, the vast majority of business managers consider computers, computer networks, and internet access to be essential business tools for recordkeeping, reporting, and communications. These tools also give the user easy access to tax information, forms, and registration with tax authorities. In fact, some tax authorities require taxpayers to complete their tax reporting and returns via their websites.

Computers are needed to operate accounting software and other tax-related software programs. Some software accounting programs include tax-related features. Others require the addition of tax modules, such as an automated process to determine the tax rate according to tax jurisdiction. If the accounting software is to be customized for the business, the business manager should ensure that any needed tax features are included. But be wary of any customization that may limit software flexibility and of computer systems that do not meet the requirements for installing and operating the software.

Most accounting software programs include features or modules for handling transactional taxes. Some include separate modules to address different state taxes and tax rates, and enable the generation of reports. Some programs will enable efficient research of tax laws, rulings, etc. Because these programs offer different features, the business manager should allow his or her tax manager(s) and/or tax experts to review each one under consideration and provide feedback.

Tax software often comes with licensing fees, update costs, and memory requirements. Some of the costs are onetime costs, whereas others are renewable or periodic. Generally, if these are not paid to procure full access, then the value of the software and computers will not be maximized and/or access will be denied.

Overall, computers, software, ISPs, and so forth are needed if the business is to effectively comply with its tax responsibilities. These tools are mostly used to manage accounting data, complete tax returns, do tax research, and communicate and share data with tax auditors. They are needed to timely provide vendors with tax exemption certificates and/or collect tax exemption certificates from customers. In effect, these tools are essential for each business.

Reference Materials

Tax reference materials, which provide information on taxes, taxability, and related topics, are available in different formats and from many different sources. Tax employees should have easy access to these materials when needed in order to maintain their level of knowledge or to efficiently perform research on tax issues.

Providers of reference materials include vendors, tax authorities, schools, professional tax service providers, and libraries. Each provider will distribute their information and knowledge using different media, including books, e-books, CDs, DVDs, articles in magazines, and websites. Others will offer seminars or tax courses via the internet or in a classroom setting.

The cost of the reference materials will depend upon the provider and how it provides its products to the recipient. Another cost impact is based on what information is being offered and the medium being used to deliver the information. Some mediums are free; some require the payment of a subscription or membership fee in order to acquire access to the information; and some require the purchase of the physical medium through which the information is shared.

Media used for sharing tax information that is available for free include the following:

- Publications
  Tax authorities offer brochures, periodicals, and other publications at no charge to the public. For these, check the tax authority's website, where you will be able to access copies or make a request for copies via mail, email, or telephone. Most of these materials may be downloaded onto your computer or printed.

- Tax rate tables
  Check online for tax authorities or other businesses that offer this data. Some tables may be in the form of a printout or a data download.

- Tax courses
  Look for seminar providers or schools that offer these tax courses for free.

- Periodical articles
  Check the internet. These may be authored by tax authorities, tax service providers, or other entities who wish to share the information with others.

- Internal resources
  Internally developed reference materials such as the business's training documents, procedures, and instructions are free of charge.

Media used for sharing tax information that is offered at a cost include the following:

- Publications
  Check bookstores and websites for sellers of any publications related to taxes.

- Tax courses
  Check with schools, tax authorities, tax professionals, and professional tax-related trade organizations and clubs.

- Tax seminars
  Check with schools, tax authorities, tax professionals, and professional tax-related trade organizations and clubs.

- Books
  Books may be procured from bookstores, online sellers, et al.

- Magazines
  Check tax-related trade magazines.

- Subscriptions
  Subscriptions to tax resources such as information-sharing websites are available for a fee.

Consideration: Be wary of outdated information or misleading information. You should check the reliability of any articles found on the internet by checking the date and place of publication. Also, look for articles from reputable businesses. But do keep in mind, even reputable businesses and tax authorities may provide outdated articles on their websites.

Subscriptions to Tax Resources

Most subscriptions give the subscriber quick and easy access to tax-related information such as tax laws, tax rulings, tax rate lookups, and tax rate files. Some allow the subscriber to ask questions, to which the subscription provider may offer information and/or guidance. The information provided is generally organized in a manner that it makes it much easier for a tax employee to complete his or her tax research.

Some providers charge a subscription fee for all or part of their services. Subscription fees will vary based on what is provided, the method of access or delivery, and/or the duration of the subscription. The most common format for delivering the information is through periodically released books and magazines and via the internet. Some subscriptions may provide a combination of these formats. Overall, the format for the delivery of the information is designed to provide specific information to the subscribers in a format that is easy to access and read.

Some subscriptions may also provide comprehensive access to information, which can become costly. These subscriptions may provide access to information for all tax jurisdictions. However, the business manager should consider minimizing costs by paying only for access to information that is directly related to his or her business and relevant tax jurisdictions.

TAX DEPARTMENTS

Tax departments are generally considered part of a business's accounting department. Its reporting structure is usually similar to other accounting departments, and it is usually placed under the direction of an accounting executive or manager such as a chief financial officer or an accounting director.

When developing a departmental budget, tax managers should include standard administrative costs similar to other accounting departments, such as their allocated share of the building rent, office furniture, office equipment, and office supplies, as well as training, salaries, and tax-related tools.

Work Space for Internal Tax Personnel

Work space and offices assigned to the tax department are part of the costs attributed to the tax department. Tax personnel should be assigned work space or offices that are located in the same building as other accounting-related departments as they should have easy access to the records and the personnel of the business departments with whom they will regularly interact. Providing this easy access will facilitate the work of the tax personnel and those they regularly work with, including people in accounting, procurement, sales, and other departments.

Other related costs will be for office furniture and the space needed for storage of documents and tools. File cabinets and/or bookcases will be needed for the storage of tax-related documents, records, and books.

The amount of work space allocated to a tax department will vary with each business. Factors to consider include budgeted monies, space, staff size, and volume of tax-related documents.

Work Space for Visiting Tax Personnel

External resources such as tax consultants and auditors may be required to work on-site at the offices of their clients. Generally, tax consultants work in an office environment, whether in their client's office building or at their own office location.

When doable, a business should allocate an office or work space for visiting tax auditors to use. This area should allow separation from the office personnel. This will allow privacy for the auditor, privacy when interacting with the auditor, and a minimal number of distractions.

As with any office personnel, when a tax consultant or auditor works on-site, he or she will need access to a table or desk, a calculator, and a copier or printer. Most tax consultants and auditors bring their own supplies and tools, such as laptops, calculators, and pens. However, do not be surprised if you find yourself providing some supplies or tools to these visitors. And when doing so, be careful about providing anything that may be misconstrued as an unauthorized gift or a bribe.

TAX POLICIES AND PROCEDURES

Every business should document its internal policies and procedures. These policies and procedures should include a section dedicated to the business's tax activities and the appropriate text for the sections dedicated to each of the other departments. Since taxes affect multiple departments, the tax manager should be able to contribute to the other departments in terms of reviewing the policies, procedures, and training they are developing.

Managers use the policies and procedures for several purposes, for example, to provide employees with official guidance and proper training on how to address taxes in terms of their area of responsibility. Policies and procedures can also be used as a baseline for auditing employee performance. This should also help to minimize errors committed by employees and increase their knowledge of the treatment of taxes in a structured manner. In effect, this will also help to minimize avoidable costs.

The process of developing and approving good policies and procedures takes time and effort. It will cost time to create, analyze, and modify the documentation. It will take time for management to review, approve, and distribute the results. However, one should always remember that the resulting product will deliver benefits if the policies and procedures are well written and, of course, are followed.

ARCHIVING TAX RECORDS

All businesses are required by law to maintain their records for a designated period of time. Each tax authority defines the statute of limitations and under what conditions tax records may be audited and be demanded. Contracts and agreements with customers and/or vendors may also include terms describing requirements for the maintenance of records for a period of time, which may differ from the requirements defined by some tax laws. For these reasons, each business must store its tax records, research materials, auditable records, tools, reference materials, etc. for the required period of time. A business also must be able to present or reproduce these items within a reasonable period of time.

A business's document retention policy should dictate the different requirements of and methods for storing tax-related records and resources. Printed reports and documents may be stored as hardcopies or may be scanned and converted to electronic files. Data records from accounting information systems can be stored using computer backups. Books are more apt to be stored in book form.

Those records and reference materials to which easy access is required are usually stored on-site and close to where the tax department is located. Some backup file cabinets and/or storage space may be located elsewhere on-site, but these are usually for older records, which are less likely to be needed.

The records that are deemed for seldom access may be stored in a warehouse designed for long-term storage. If the business has allocated space for such a warehouse, it may be at the same location as the tax department. Or these records may be shipped to an off-site document warehouse.

Document warehouses can be rented or leased from a business that offers to store and protect archived documents and electronic backups of computer files. Regardless of what is to be archived, the warehouse should be able to protect all the records from the environment and from events such as fires, pipe leaks, pest infestation, and unauthorized access.

Business managers must consider the costs to archive, store, and retrieve these records. They must also consider the costs to reproduce the records in the required format and in a timely manner. Such capability will vary according to the packages offered, competition, and the available storage and warehousing space owned by the business.

CONTRACTS AND OTHER LEGAL CONSIDERATIONS

Businesses that use written contracts and agreements in conjunction with their transactions should consider including tax-related terms and conditions in these documents to ensure that the tax-related responsibilities of each party are clearly defined. This will help to minimize confusion and disagreements between buyers and sellers. It will also allow the parties to define their own terms and set their own conditions for their transactions.

Contracts and agreements, which are used to record the legal responsibilities that have been agreed upon between two or more parties, must adhere to applicable statutes, judicial rulings, and other legal regulations. In effect, these are legally binding, except for any part that is found to be unenforceable. When tax-related terms and conditions are not specifically listed in contracts, the parties involved are obligated to adhere to active statutes, judicial rulings, implied contractual terms, and/or the Uniform Commercial Code of the United States (UCC) or another, similar code.

Terms and Conditions

Including tax-related terms and conditions in contracts and agreements has multifold benefits and purposes. Such a contract may be used to describe or reiterate, in layman's language, the legal tax responsibilities imposed upon each of the participating parties. Or it may be used to remind each party of their tax responsibilities. It may also define specific actions required of each party that are not listed in statutes, judicial rulings, etc. And it can be used to define the indemnification format for the resolution of unpaid taxes, penalties, interest, and other such costs related to taxes.

Excluding tax-related terms and conditions from contracts may expose the parties to undesirable results, unnecessary costs, and confusion. This is especially true for complicated transactions. First, the tax responsibilities revert to those described by established tax laws, judicial rulings, the UCC, and so forth. Second, this may cause unexpected confusion as to who pays which taxes and which taxes are reimbursable. A disagreement regarding taxes may lead to mediation with a third party or agency that may be able to impose its influence upon any resolution.

Some standardized contract forms may be procured online or at brick-and-mortar stores. These generally contain standard terms and conditions that may be used for uncomplicated transactions. However, they may be too generic to protect the parties involved and may need some customization. In such cases where generic forms are used, you should add the necessary terms and conditions to ensure the appropriate protection.

Emphasis: It is important to understand that some buyers and sellers do *not* understand tax laws, tax responsibilities, and/or applicable tax rates. Terms and conditions should be used to supplement the knowledge of the parties involved.

Business and contract managers should consider the following when designing a contract with any tax-related terms and conditions:

Issuance and delivery of applicable exemption certificates must be done in a timely manner or else taxes will be billed.

Indemnification for sellers when a buyer provides an exemption certificate that is found to be invalid by a tax authority. The contract should address the reimbursement of costs, such as taxes, penalties, and interest, that the seller was required to pay because of a fault of the buyer.

The buyer is responsible for any taxes on items or services he or she provides to a seller for use by the seller in completing his or her deliverables. Example: the buyer pays taxes on two pieces of pipe, which are given to the seller to weld together. This will help to clarify who is responsible for the taxes of the items provided and will minimize costs and any confusion associated with applicable use taxes.

Whether taxes shall be listed on invoices separately from the price of the items sold. This will help to clearly identify whether applicable transactional taxes are included in the selling price or the amount billed.

Whether the seller shall print a statement on his or her invoice(s) to clarify whether any transactional tax is included in the amount billed.

Resolution of tax-related liens, including how they are to be resolved and by whom. This may occur when the seller or his or her subcontractor fails to properly address his or her tax responsibilities.

Record retention. Parties shall retain transaction-related records and documents at least for as long as required by tax laws or as long as is mutually agreed. Most contracts should ask for at least five years of retention. Larger companies may ask for a longer retention time.

Hierarchy of contractual documents. There are times when the terminology of one agreement may contradict that of another. Adding text for this type of situation should help to identify which documents have precedence over the other documents.

Hierarchy of Contracts

Sometimes, more than one legal document may be issued for a business relationship and/or associated transactions between the participating parties. When this occurs, terms and conditions may be introduced that override the terms and conditions of another document. Along with this, there is also the possibility that some of the terms and conditions within a document will contradict other terms and conditions within that same document. And there may be some confusion regarding which document has precedence over the other document(s). All of these situations may lead to confusion and costly consequences for one or both of the parties involved.

In order to minimize confusion and costs resulting from contradicting legal documents, the parties should consider including a clause to their contract(s) to clearly describe the hierarchy or order of precedence of contracts and related documents. This hierarchy should clearly define which document takes precedence over or overrides the other. It should also identify and/or describe the legal documents to be used. If a clarifying clause is not included in the contract and there is a discrepancy about the terms and conditions, the parties risk having to refer the issue to a third-party arbitration process and/or seek other legal remedy.

The following commonly contain tax-related terms and conditions:

- master contract
- master service agreement
- contract
- contract amendment

- bid request
- quote
- estimate

- purchase order
- sales order
- change order
- work order
- release order.

Lawsuits

Lawsuits may be initiated as a result of unsettled issues related to transactional taxes or noncompliance with the contract(s). Depending on the terms and conditions of the contracts involved, a lawsuit may be settled by arbitration or via the courts. Rulings may be appealed, and some appeals may result in a trial by a higher court. Sometimes, the case will be taken all the way through the court system to be heard by the Supreme Court of the United States.

Some tax lawsuits are initiated as a result of assessments from a tax audit that the taxpayer does not agree with. Some lawsuits may be initiated as a way to protest a new tax law or changes to an existing one. Also, lawsuits may be initiated when, in a commercial transaction, tax-related issues have brought harm to a buyer and/or seller.

The rulings from a court or tax board are used to resolve a case in progress and are made available to other taxpayers and tax authorities for purposes of clarifying certain aspects of their own cases. The sharing of information associated with these rulings is required by law, as a matter of public record. One way that tax authorities provide such access is via their websites. Other organizations may share the information for a fee or at no cost, but accompanied by advertisements.

Regardless of the basis of a tax-related lawsuit, it should be taken seriously. Lawsuits have a direct effect on the litigants and require further action from one or more of the litigants. Some lawsuits will also make an indirect impact on other taxpayers and litigants who are working with similar cases or situations. Some taxpayers and tax authorities may derive guidance and/or clarification of tax laws, and the ruling may reiterate a position taken by the taxpayer(s) or tax authority.

CIVIL AND CRIMINAL LITIGATION

When a tax authority accuses a taxpayer of not complying with tax laws, the taxpayer may be exposed to penalties and legal procedures, which may include court orders, civil charges, and/or criminal charges. When more serious in nature, most of these require some type of defensive action by the litigant or the accused, including the hiring of tax lawyers or other authorized representatives.

Civil penalties are usually less serious and less costly than criminal charges, but civil penalties may become extremely costly—and they are generally avoidable.

Civil penalties usually result from actions that may include the following:

- failure to file a return in a timely manner
- failure to pay taxes reported on a return
- omission of taxes required to be shown on the return
- failure to make records available in an auditable form to tax auditors
- failure to make or maintain records, or make the records available to an agent of a tax authority
- failure to collect taxes from buyers and remit them when due
- selling untaxed liquor, motor fuel, or cigarettes
- issuance of a false or fraudulent exemption certificate.

Criminal charges for tax-related acts, such as tax evasion or tax fraud, are more serious and can result in a prison sentence as a penalty. Although it is possible that some of these charges may be the result of innocent negligence or ignorance, proving one's innocence may be challenging.

Tax-related criminal charges may result from the more serious actions, which may include any of the following:

- failure to file a return
- failure to report total revenue
- failure to collect sales taxes as required by tax authorities
- failure to remit all tax monies collected from buyers
- selling untaxed liquor, motor fuel, or cigarettes
- signing a false tax return
- falsifying or altering documents
- willful failure to keep required records.

Because there are variations in the tax laws between different tax jurisdictions, taxpayers need to be become familiar with the tax laws of the jurisdictions in which they will complete business transactions.

SUMMARY

Business managers should keep in mind how costs associated with taxes will affect their budgets, their expenditures, and the profits of the business. Tax-related costs may be either direct or indirect. Some of these costs may arise well after the initial transaction is completed.

Tax-related costs and considerations are affected by the management of the business and by its policies and procedures, tax-related tools, and personnel. How these are addressed is similar to the way other business segments address them, but with a different goal. However, the success of achieving tax-related goals will depend upon management's understanding, strategies, and intention to achieve these goals.

Changes in tax laws will also affect tax costs and the terms and conditions related to tax management in any written agreement. If the appropriate tax-related terms and conditions are not included in agreements, this may lead to confusion and unnecessary costs.

Chapter 10

Tax Compliance Goals

Most business managers recognize that in order to facilitate and maximize tax compliance, they need to identify, establish, and use a complementary system of tax goals, tools, and resources. These managers must identify the ultimate tax goal and then acquire and use the appropriate tools and resources to achieve it. Afterward, the manager should periodically review and update these goals, tools, and resources as needed, similar to any project management.

One would think that 100 percent tax compliance is the ultimate tax goal, and indeed such is possible under ideal conditions and with ideal resources. However, the possibility of achieving 100 percent tax compliance is a daunting task, especially when human beings are involved or when the tools and resources they have available are not the best for the job.

Identifying and setting goals is a critical part of the strategy for achieving the desired level of tax compliance. Conscious consideration and identification of the steps, tools, and resources is imperative as it will facilitate the monitoring of progress and the identification of any deviation from the ultimate goal. More importantly, this consideration will increase the chances of success in achieving the desired level of tax compliance.

The following list may be used to help identify and set tax compliance goals. Each of these steps is elaborated upon hereafter.

- Identify and prioritize goals.
- Develop a schedule for completing the goals.
- Identify participants and their roles and contributions.
- Identify technical tools and resources.
- Regularly assess the progress toward the completion of each goal.

- Adjust goals, schedules, and priorities as needed.
- Acquire management's approval as needed.
- Provide oversight of work compliance.

Consideration: A realistic tax compliance goal should read similar to this: To maximize tax compliance and, meanwhile, efficiently and effectively address all tax responsibilities and minimize tax costs.

IDENTIFY AND PRIORITIZE GOALS

For any tax related project, in order to develop a good strategy, you should start with identifying the ultimate goal you want to achieve. In most cases, this goal will be to maximize tax compliance within an identified scope. For a newly formed business, the scope will likely include all business procedures affected by taxes. For an established business, the scope will likely be limited to addressing a weakness in a specific business procedure, such as resolving the repeated billing of improper taxes to customers. After identifying the ultimate goal, you will need to identify the strategy to accomplish this. In general, the scope of the ultimate goal and of the subgoals will vary depending upon the needs of the business, authorizations, budgets, and such.

Identifying subgoals and prioritizing them is the next step after the identification of the ultimate goal. A subgoal is basically a specific step that must be completed in order to achieve the ultimate goal. The number and the tier levels of any subgoals will depend upon an understanding of the business, organizational skills, and the overall scope and depth of the project.

Each of the subgoals will surely have subgoals, and it is possible that these lower-tier goals will have subgoals that also have subgoals. The number of tiers of subgoals for a project will depend on various factors, including the following:

- whether or not the project is adjusting present procedures or starting new tax procedures,
- how detailed oriented the project manager is, and
- what tools and resources are available and will be used.

Emphasis: All goals should be clear and achievable, including the primary and all lower-tiered goals. They should be identified, measurable, and trackable, and they should be regularly monitored for progress and any needed modifications.

Following is an example of a high-level list of goals with the ultimate goal and the first tier of subgoals. It does not include the lower tiers of subgoals, which are required to complete the first tier of subgoals.

Sample Set of Tax Goals

Ultimate goal   Maximize tax compliance, meanwhile efficiently and effectively addressing all tax responsibilities and minimizing tax costs.

Subgoals   Identify and prioritize subgoals.
Develop a schedule for completing the goals.
Identify participants, roles, and contributions.
Identify technical tools and resources.
Regularly assess the progress of each goal toward completion.
Adjust goals, schedules, and priority as needed.
Acquire management's approval as needed.
Implement new processes and procedures.

DEVELOP A SCHEDULE FOR COMPLETING THE GOALS

Goals and subgoals should be initiated and completed in an organized manner. Time lines and strategies should be used when striving to achieve any tax compliance goal. Personnel, tools, and resources will have to be made available and scheduled for use. Progress should be regularly monitored to determine whether to rearrange the schedule of tasks or goals. In effect, all these components should be coordinated.

At the start of each project, each subgoal should be reviewed sufficiently to be able to determine an estimated start time and how long the goal will take to complete. This information will allow for the development of a reasonable time line.

Because some lower-tier goals may have to be completed sequentially or concurrently with other subgoals, someone has to determine when to start or postpone each subgoal. This will allow the project to be organized and the progress to be measureable. Doing this will help to keep the subgoals on track and keep the entire project on schedule.

Estimated time lines are also needed in order to identify the time line for acquiring and employing the needed tools, resources, financing, budgets, and approvals. Coordinating tasks with tools, resources, etc., can be a challenge for some organizations. For this, it is best to be proactive, or the success of the project may be at risk.

Emphasis: The more organized the project is, the more efficient and successful it will be.

IDENTIFY PARTICIPANTS AND THEIR ROLES AND CONTRIBUTIONS

Participants who will complete the tasks and subgoals must be identified and then assigned roles to play and contributions to make. But before selecting participants and assigning the roles and contributions, managers should verify whether the participants are sufficiently qualified and have enough experience to complete their assignments. If they are not qualified, they should be trained or replaced with better-qualified participants.

Participants should either have enough time available to contribute to achieving the goals or change the priorities of their responsibilities. Depending on the goals and subgoals, some participants may be able to take on more than one role and, in effect, contribute to different deliverables.

Some of the participants include the following:

Managers, who will manage the goals, tasks, and scheduling. Managers will also manage and oversee the personnel, tax consultants, et al.

Approvers, who will authorize costs, strategies, goals, etc.

Trainers, who will train others on the implementation of new tax procedures, new tools, and other tax-related components.

Trainees, who will employ the new procedures, software, tools, etc., as part of their revised job duties.

Tax consultants, who will advise others on software, tools, procedures, etc.

Clerical personnel, who will do simple tasks such as data entry, organizing documents, collecting missing information, and acquiring documents.

Tax software analyzers, who will help other employees understand how to use any software or will help with the analysis, design, and/or implementation of any software.

Computer technicians, who will implement software, needed hardware, and/or network infrastructure.

Buyers, who may conduct research, process purchase requisitions, and/or place orders for tools, software, resources, etc.

Emphasis: As with any schedule and time line, the participants, their roles, and their contributions should be monitored. If need be, tasks should be adjusted in order to ensure that a qualified person is working on the subgoal for which he or she is the best match.

IDENTIFY TECHNICAL TOOLS AND RESOURCES

Information technology, a tool that may be used to facilitate tax compliance, includes software, computers, the internet, accounting software, G/L coding structure, tax coding structures, data collection software, and reports. Subscriptions that give a user access to tax information are also important resources for tax compliance. Most companies will use some combination of these tools when they start their business activities, and some will refine the implementation of these tools as needed and as their managers become more familiar with their tax compliance needs and the tools to meet them.

Because of the different technical tools and resources available for tax management, subgoals should be set to identify, evaluate, and select relevant software, computer equipment, and related resources. If software is to be implemented, then a subgoal should be set to configure the software and implement it for use. Along with software, it necessary to acquire and configure hardware and related resources.

Before any software may be used, participants who have the technical skills and experience to do so should be assigned to install it and configure it. Consider using consultants and tax experts for this task, as they will help to ensure that the information systems are capable and sufficient for the needs of the business. The responsibilities assigned to these technical consultants and tax experts will vary according to the company that hires them. They may be asked to determine whether the tools on hand are sufficient to generate the needed data and/or reports; to analyze the data needed for compliance or to provide strategies for doing so; or to work with other personnel.

Trainers will be needed to train the business's employees. Managers should make an effort to ensure that these trainers are sufficiently familiar or experienced with the tools and with transactional taxes to train others.

Managers should determine whether to use trainers for all training sessions or only selected topics and/or provide training manuals. Some trainers may be asked to train a select group of personnel or all personnel on the new information system or procedures. At the least, the trainer should be expected to provide training manuals and tools.

Emphasis: Do not expect untrained or minimally experienced employees to be highly efficient in completing their tax-related tasks.

REGULARLY ASSESS THE PROGRESS TOWARD EACH GOAL

Throughout the project, monitor the progress toward each subgoal in order to identify any weaknesses and strengths and to determine whether there is a need to change the schedule, the priorities, the coordination of personnel, the tools, and/or other resources. This will involve the regular monitoring of ongoing tasks and identifying whether deliverables are taking longer to complete than expected.

Tip: If the project is complicated, the project leaders should consider using project management software to facilitate the monitoring of the progress, scheduling, etc.

If the progress toward completion is slower than expected or is delayed, a manager should review the situation, identify the reason(s) for the delay, and identify a remedy to address the delay. Once a remedy has been identified, it should be presented for approval and incorporated into the present schedule.

If a remedy does not fit the needs of the project, then cease using it.

Some subgoals may have to be eliminated or adjusted. A subgoal should not be considered complete unless its completion has been validated and its deliverables have been found to be adequate or acceptable. A manager should sign off on each subgoal.

ADJUST GOALS, SCHEDULES, AND PRIORITIES AS NEEDED

After identifying the initial goals and organizing them into an initial project plan, do not be surprised if you find you need to add more goals and/or modify the project plan. It is OK if you have to make these types of adjustments, although it may be challenging if these adjustments end up being significant, which would mean that the plan and goals were not sufficiently considered. But all is not lost. You can add to or modify the goals in order to achieve your intended results. After all, it is your project.

Emphasis: Do not hesitate to adjust goals, schedules, and priorities.

ACQUIRE MANAGEMENT'S APPROVAL AS NEEDED

All goals, subgoals, and tasks associated with tax compliance should be reviewed and approved by the appropriate manager. This usually occurs at the start of any project, as the project progresses, and of course at the end.

Depending on the business's structure, you may need approval from one or more levels. First approval will likely be to acknowledge and initiate the strategy for the ultimate goal. Then, depending on the scope and subgoals of the strategy, there will be costs and budgets to consider. There will be policies and procedures to implement and/or modify. Along with the strategy, there will be resources to allocate and expend.

Some managers hire tax consultants or experienced tax experts to oversee or assist with verification of the deliverables. Other managers may already be sufficiently experienced and knowledgeable with regard to the goals or will make an effort to educate themselves or their staff as needed.

OVERSIGHT OF WORK COMPLIANCE

After the policies and procedures are revised, there should be some oversight and monitoring scheduled to ensure that employees understand the changes and are adhering to them. This oversight will also enable the overseer to identify employee weaknesses and strengths resulting from the recent changes, which will empower managers to address these in a timely manner.

Perform a statistical study to identify weaknesses and strengths. Observe how many errors are made, in what area, and by whom.

Afterward, determine what is needed to increase compliance. It may be a matter of more training or the clarification of policies and/or procedures. It may require adjustments to the policy or procedures. Software may need to be reconfigured, or an untrainable employee or one who does not care to do the work requested of him or her needs to be removed from a team.

The oversight should be performed at regular intervals in order to timely identify weaknesses and strengths and to timely address them.

SUMMARY

In order to achieve the desired level of tax compliance, a business must identify and act upon several strategies.

A department devoted to tax compliance should be treated similarly to other business departments. Each business should identify what it takes to be compliant. Based on this, the management should set goals, monitor progress, and makes changes as needed. Management should also set up the appropriate processes and procedures, use adequate tools, and train the personnel.

A business has a constant need to monitor, update, and modify the resources, tools, and staff it employs. Before any major changes are made in terms of resources or tools, the business should perform research and analysis, and employ decision-making skills. These changes should follow the concept of project management. In other words, a systematic approach to achieving the ultimate goal of tax compliance is always necessary.

Chapter 11

Personal Transactions

Many noncommercial buyers and sellers are minimally familiar with transactional taxes and with how these taxes may affect their personal transactions. Some may not be aware of, or may minimize, the fact that noncommercial consumers are held responsible for paying transactional taxes when required by law. Many may feel confident that the seller will bill the appropriate taxes, or they may think that the tax doesn't apply to them. Regardless of the different views on transactional taxes, most consumers spend little time considering their own compliance with tax responsibilities when they are making personal purchases and sales.

Purchases intended for personal use *do* require compliance with transactional tax laws, similar to what is required of commercial businesses. These taxes are imposed and treated in a similar way as taxes on commercial transactions. The buyers in this case will be held responsible for paying taxes when due, remitting use taxes, and so on. In effect, buyers need to be as aware of tax-related considerations when making purchases intended for personal use, similar to commercial buyers when making business-related purchases.

In general, consumers should keep in mind that purchases intended for their own personal use or consumption may be classified as either taxable or nontaxable. Exemptions may be available for certain transactions. Sometimes sellers may fail to bill the appropriate taxes on their invoices. With these considerations in mind, a wise and ethical consumer should be aware of these possibilities and put forth the appropriate effort to comply his or her their tax responsibilities.

TAXABLE PERSONAL TRANSACTIONS

Taxes on most transactions where the items procured are for personal consumption, storage, use, or transference as a gift are imposed upon the retail price or value of the goods and services procured. However, the actual tax and the imposed rate will depend upon the item procured and where the sale is completed.

Note: There is a difference between personal consumption, storage, and use. However, in the end, the items are usually deemed taxable—and at the same tax rate.

Personal consumption involves the noncommercial use of the item procured. These items, usually called consumables, include goods and services. They differ from personal use items in that they are consumed (are used up or become nonusable after the initial use, as opposed to be used repeatedly).

Some examples of items that are procured as consumables are as follows:

- Band-Aids
- bath soap
- body wash
- cable service
- candles
- electricity
- fertilizer
- hairspray

- ice cream
- deodorant
- dry-cleaning services
- leasing
- makeup
- nail polish
- natural gas
- paint
- paper

- pencils
- pens
- pesticide
- rug cleaning services
- rental
- shaving cream
- soft drinks
- suntan lotion.

Caveat: The list of items classified as consumables in one jurisdiction may be different in another.

Personal storage involves items that are procured and stored as they are intended, not for immediate use, but for use in the future. These items may also be known as spare parts or supplies. The concept here is similar to the storing of inventory items.

Some examples of taxable purchases for storage are as follows:

- air conditioner filters
- light bulbs
- auto parts for future auto maintenance
- nails for future projects.

These items are usually taxable at the time of purchase, and usually there is no exemption available for this type of purchase as the items are ultimately for personal use and not commercial use.

Personal use applies when items are procured for use in a noncommercial or noncharitable activity. These items may or may not be consumed, used up, or destroyed upon their initial use. In fact, these items can be used repeatedly.

Some examples of items that are procured for personal use are as follows:

- appliances
- barbecue grills
- chairs
- clothing
- computers
- lamps
- magazines
- motor oil
- schoolbooks
- stoves
- sunglasses
- tables
- televisions
- tools
- vacuum cleaner.

Transference of gifts includes the procurement of items that are intended to be given as a gift. Usually, the person who procures these items will pay the applicable transactional taxes. If the taxes are not paid at the time of purchase, then the end user or recipient may be designated as the ultimate user and will be held responsible for paying any applicable use or consumption taxes.

NONTAXABLE PERSONAL TRANSACTIONS

Most tax authorities have identified exceptions to the taxation of some personal-related transactions. These exceptions usually apply to items that are necessary for living, as opposed to nonessential items. No tax is charged to either the buyer or the user for these items, and usually no exemption certificate or declaration is required.

Some of the exceptions to taxable personal use items are as follows:

- unprocessed foods
- medical services
- newspapers
- occasional sales
- prescribed medications
- professional services
- exports.

OTHER PERSONAL TRANSACTIONS

Be aware of purchases that may be misconstrued to fall into the category of either a taxable or nontaxable personal transaction. More specifically, watch for items that are normally taxable when sold at retail but are deemed nontaxable when sold during certain situations, such as the occasional sale transaction or when the product is for exportation.

Occasional sales are sales by a seller who is not in the business of selling and does not sell the item(s) on a regular basis. For this type of transaction, the seller may be required to complete a tax form to declare that the sale was an occasional sale. An example of such an occasional sale is when a person sells one of his personal automobiles (and only one) within a twelve-month period. Another example of occasional sales is an annual garage sale.

There are limitations on how many of such sales are considered to qualify as occasional sales before the seller no longer fits the classification of an occasional sales seller. It could be as few as two sales within a twelve-month period.

Export transactions may also be deemed nontaxable if the items are exported out of the tax jurisdictions. An exception to this is when a tax agreement requires the seller to collect from the buyer any transactional taxes imposed by the destination tax jurisdiction. Usually, if the seller does not have nexus in the destination tax jurisdiction, he or she will *not* be required to collect those taxes. However, be wary as laws are changing and some jurisdictions may require the seller to charge and collect transactional taxes and remit them to the destination tax jurisdiction.

EXEMPTIONS FOR PERSONAL TRANSACTIONS

Yes, there are exemptions available for some personal transactions that are outside the norm. These exemptions are intended to encourage purchases, provide financial assistance to the public, encourage energy conservation, encourage charity contributions, and so forth. In general, these exemptions are granted with the purpose of helping society. However, be aware that some of these exemptions may be temporary. As soon as society no longer needs this assistance, these exemptions will surely cease.

To be granted some personal exemptions, the taxpayer may be required to complete exemption certification forms. These tax exemptions are provided by the taxing authority, who also provides information about the exemption and its scope. Taxpayers should check with the relevant taxing authority to learn what is required for them to declare an exemption and whether there are time restrictions.

Below, you will find descriptions of exemptions available for personal transactions. These include the following:

- back-to-school tax exemptions
- conservation-related tax exemptions
- charity-related tax exemptions
- severe weather and emergency preparedness tax exemptions
- disaster-related tax exemptions
- other tax exemptions.

Back-to-School Tax Exemptions

These exemptions, which may also be known as back-to-school holidays or sales tax holidays, are designed to allow the tax-free purchase of certain school-related items within a specific time period and within a value range. Each of these exemptions is legislatively authorized by the appropriate tax authority.

Back-to-school exemptions apply to necessary school-related items such as clothes, shoes, and classroom supplies below a stated dollar amount.

Basically, the exemption is intended for items necessary for school, not for items such as luxury clothing.

Taxing authorities define a specific period of time for when these exemptions are in effect, usually on a weekend and within a month or two before the start of the new school year. Reminders of these exemptions are shared by some local news media. Check with your taxing authority for details. Upon the approval of back-to-school exemptions each year, the tax authority will publicize the eligible items and when they must be purchased to receive the exemption.

Generally, back-to-school transactions do not require an exemption certification form. Instead, sellers are held responsible for not charging tax on the exempted items unless they have opted out from the tax holiday.

Listed in table 11.1 are states that have enacted a back-to-school exemption holiday, along with the dates for the year 2022 and the related tax code excerpt or interpretation.

Taxpayers should keep in mind that these laws vary as they are enacted by the different jurisdictions. Also, because of the possibility of a change to the laws, the dates may vary from year to year, or the tax jurisdiction may decide to void the exemption altogether. Some states that have not yet enacted any such laws may choose to do so.

State	Period	Tax code excerpt and interpretation
Alabama	July 15–17	Begins at 12:01 a.m. on the third Friday in July, and ends at 12:00 midnight on the following Sunday, pursuant to 40-23-210 through 213, Code of Alabama.
Arkansas	August 6–7	Act 757 of 2011 provides for a sales tax holiday in Arkansas during the first weekend of August each year.
Connecticut	August 21–27	The "sales tax holiday" occurs the third Sunday in August through the following Saturday.
Iowa	August 5–6	Iowa Code section 423.3(68)(a)(2) states the sales tax holiday begins at 12:01 a.m. on the first Friday in August and ends at 12:00 midnight the following day.

Maryland	August 14–20	From 12:01 a.m. on the second Sunday in August through midnight on the following Saturday
Massachusetts	Pending resolution	M.G.L.c. 64H, §6A provides for a Massachusetts "sales tax holiday weekend," which will occur annually, on a two-day weekend designated by the general court by joint resolution no later than June 15. If the general court fails to adopt such a joint resolution, the Commissioner of Revenue shall, no later than July 1, designate a two-day weekend in August of that year as the annual sales tax holiday.
Mississippi	July 29–30	2010 MS Code: 27-65-111(bb). Sale takes place during a period beginning at 12:01 a.m. on the last Friday in July and ending at 12:00 midnight the following Saturday.
Oklahoma	August 5–7	Beginning at 12:01 a.m. on the first Friday in August and ending at 12:00 midnight on the following Sunday. OAC 710:65-13-511(a).
South Carolina	August 5–7	South Carolina Code §12-36-2120(57) provides for an annual three-day "sales tax holiday" beginning 12:01 a.m. on the first Friday in August and ending at 12:00 midnight the following Sunday.
Tennessee	July 29–31	The sales tax holiday begins the last Friday in July each year at 12:01 a.m. and ends at 11:59 p.m. the following Sunday. TN Code Ann. § 67-6-393.
Texas	April 23–25	The period that begins on Friday before the fifteenth day preceding the fourth Monday in August, and ends at 12:00 a.m. (midnight) on the following Sunday. Rule § 3.365.
Virginia	August 5–7	The three-day sales tax holiday begins the first Friday in August and ends the following Sunday each year.

TABLE 11.1. Back-to-school tax holidays.

Conservation-Related Tax Exemptions

Conservation-related tax exemptions, which may also be known as Energy Star sales tax holidays, are intended to be an incentive to purchase energy-efficient products. As such, it is predominantly available for items that meet the federal Energy Star requirements.

Energy Star products are designed to be energy-efficient. The Energy Star program, operated by the United States Environmental Protection Agency and the United States Department of Energy, formally designates a product as being energy-efficient, which is indicated by a label with the Energy Star logo.

Products that qualify for this exemption include designated air conditioners, refrigerators, ceiling fans, incandescent and fluorescent light bulbs, dishwashers, clothes washers, and dehumidifiers. Some nonqualifying items include water heaters, clothes dryers, freezers, stoves, attic fans, and heat pumps.

Limitations placed on the conservation-related exemption generally relate to price or to the total value of the products or number of products. Look for any limitations on what counts as a qualifying product.

Usually, a taxpayer does not need an exemption certificate or other certification document in order to claim this exemption. Also, this exemption may apply to local taxes.

Some states that enacted conservation-related exemptions in 2022 include Maryland, Texas, and Virginia.

State	Period	Tax code excerpt and interpretation
Maryland	February 19–21	Between 12:01 a.m. on the Saturday immediately preceding the third Monday in February and 11:59 p.m. on the third Monday of February.
Texas	May 28–30	The period beginning at 12:01 a.m. on the Saturday preceding the last Monday in May (Memorial Day) and ending at 11:50 p.m. on the last Monday in May. Rule 3.369.
Virginia	August 5–7	The Three-day sales tax holiday starts the first Friday in August at 12:01 a.m. and ends the following Sunday at 11:59 p.m.

TABLE 11.2. Conservation-related tax exemptions.

Charity-Related Tax Exemptions

When an individual purchases, rents, or leases a taxable item for the purpose of donating that item to an exempt organization, he or she may be able to declare an exemption from transactional taxes. The individual should check with the relevant tax authority in order to determine the taxability of such procurements, any related limitations, and any available exemptions. The individual should also check for the forms he or she must complete in order to take advantage of the exemptions.

Individuals should keep in mind that they may not be able to use the charity-related exemption if the item was used prior to being donated to a tax-exempt entity. If the item was indeed used beforehand, then it will not be considered a donated item. In effect, it will be considered a personal purchase that was used (which is a taxable event) and then gifted. However, if the item was used for the end purpose of donating it to an exempt organization without anyone's having used it for personal reasons, then the charity-related exemption may apply. An example of this type of use is when the item procured is incorporated into, or used to make, another item of value that is donated to an exempt organization.

Severe Weather and Emergency Preparedness Tax Exemptions

A severe weather and emergency preparedness tax exemption may also be known as a severe weather holiday or emergency preparedness sales tax holiday. These exemptions are designed to encourage people to stock up on emergency-related supplies in preparation for severe weather. The exemptions will be available on specified days, and limits are placed on the dollar value of the items to which the exemptions apply. In general, these exemptions are usually authorized by tax authorities whose jurisdictions are regularly affected by severe weather.

States that enacted a severe weather-related exemption in 2022 include Alabama, Florida, Texas, and Virginia.

State	Period	Tax code excerpt and interpretation
Alabama	February 25–27	Beginning at 12:01 a.m. on Friday of the last full weekend in February and ending at 12:00 midnight on the following Sunday, pursuant to 40-23-230 through 233, Code of Alabama 1975.
Florida	May 28–June 10	*Note:* Legislation is passed on an annual basis. Rule: 12AER22-3 Sales Tax Holiday for Disaster Preparedness Supplies during the Period of May 28, 2022 through June 10, 2022.
Texas	April 23–25	The period beginning at 12:01 a.m. on the Saturday before the last Monday in April and ending at 12:00 midnight on the last Monday in April.
Virginia	August 5–7	The three-day sales tax holiday starts the first Friday in August at 12:01 a.m. and ends the following Sunday at 11:59 p.m.

TABLE 11.3. Severe weather sales tax exemptions for personal purchases.

Items that qualify for severe weather preparedness exemptions usually include the following:

- certain batteries, for example, batteries for cellular phones or flashlights
- cell phone chargers
- self-contained first aid kits
- self-powered or battery-powered radios
- portable generators
- self-powered or battery-powered light sources
- duct tape
- materials designed to protect window openings, for example, plywood and window film
- nonelectric food storage cooler
- water storage container
- nonelectric can opener
- fire extinguisher, smoke detector, carbon monoxide detector
- gas or diesel fuel containers
- ground anchor systems and tie-down kits
- tools such as hatchets and axes
- tarps and other plastic sheeting.

Usually, exemptions for items related to severe weather preparedness will *not* apply to items such as the following:

- batteries for cars, boats, or other motorized vehicles
- camping stoves and camping supplies
- chain saws.

Along with the limitations on the type of items that qualify, there are limitations on the time period during which these exemptions are available, usually two or three days. Of course, there are also limitations placed on the dollar value of the purchased items in order to exclude nonessential items from this exemption.

For other information about these exemptions, check with the taxing authority that enacted the exemptions. The easiest way to do this is to check the tax authority's website.

Disaster-Related Exemptions

Some tax authorities will make exemptions available for purchases of items used to help with disaster recovery. These exemptions are intended to provide some financial relief for those who are affected by the disaster, which in turn will help the whole community to recover from the disaster.

Disaster-related exemptions are usually enacted just before or right after a disaster occurs, or after an official declaration of a state of disaster has been made. Usually, tax authorities will move to enact these exemptions in a timely manner.

The exemption legislation will identify items that qualify for the exemption as well as provide time limitations and discuss other related requirements. Buyers should check with their tax authorities to discover whether their transaction will qualify for tax-exempt status because of the disaster and whether they will have to complete any exemption certification form or declaration document.

Other Tax Exemptions

Some other, lesser-known exemptions are also made available for noncommercial purchases. These exemptions are usually intended to aid specific activities or interests, and because of this, they are more limited than those previously described. Check with the relevant tax authority for a list of these exemptions, their limitations, and their scope.

Some of the lesser-known exemptions, which apply to the procurement of goods and services, are as follows:

Gun safes and safety devices. This exemption was enacted by Tennessee, and it applies to specified items sold at retail during the tax holiday period beginning July 1, 2021, and ending June 30, 2022.

Veteran disability exemptions are allowed by certain states and vary by state. Differences include the exemption scope and the items that qualify.

> *Note:* A prerequisite for a veteran who wishes to take advantage of this exemption may be that he or she became disabled during actual military service.

Exemptions for people with disabilities are given to people with disabilities so they may procure certain items and services without having to pay transactional taxes, which may include motor vehicle sales taxes.

> This exemption covers some items for which a buyer may be required to provide a prescription or an exemption certificate to the seller. Other items may be specifically exempted by law, and therefore the buyer does not need to present a prescription or exemption certificate to the seller. The exemption may also apply to services such as repairs, maintenance, or modification of the exempted item(s).

> Check with the relevant tax jurisdiction(s) in order to learn what items qualify for this exemption and whether any limitations are imposed.

REFUNDS

If a buyer mistakenly pays too much tax on a transaction, he or she may request a refund from either the seller (the most common situation) or the relevant tax authority. If the seller, for whatever reason, refuses to refund the tax monies, the buyer may request the refund from the relevant tax authority. Usually, it is a lot easier to try to collect the refund from the seller. But the buyer should not accept a refund from both the seller and the tax authority. It must be from one or the other.

When requesting a refund from a seller, a buyer will either have to (1) explain the basis for the refund request or (2) present a valid exemption certificate. To make the refund request from a tax authority, the buyer submits the applicable tax form the next tax reporting period.

Tax jurisdictions place a time limit of three or four years on a taxpayer's request for a refund. Taxpayers should keep this in mind.

For more information on refunds, check with the relevant tax authorities.

USE TAXES

Use tax is similar to sales tax. If a buyer is unable to pay the applicable sales tax to a seller, he or she may be held responsible for paying use taxes on that transaction directly to the tax authority. In effect, the buyer is responsible for remitting use taxes to the appropriate tax authority unless he or she is able to take advantage of an exemption.

Most responsible buyers prefer to have sellers bill the appropriate sales taxes on any taxable transactions. However, sometimes the seller is not authorized or required to bill the buyer for these sales taxes.

For the form required to report and remit use taxes, the buyer should check with the relevant tax authority. This form may be named Individual Use Tax Return, or Sales and Use Tax Return, or something similar.

A buyer is apt to encounter a seller who does not or cannot bill the appropriate sales taxes in the following situations:

- A transaction with a seller who is not registered or is not located in the tax jurisdiction where the purchased products are to be delivered.

  The buyer should check with the seller to determine whether he or she is authorized to collect transactional taxes for the delivery point. If the seller is not registered or is unauthorized, the buyer will have to remit the use taxes to the appropriate tax authority.

- Internet or online purchases

  When purchases are made and the seller is neither located nor registered in the destination jurisdiction, the buyer should remit applicable use taxes to the tax authority of the destination jurisdiction.

- Imports

  Sellers delivering an item imported from a location outside the United States' borders should check to determine whether the importing entity is authorized to collect and remit transactional taxes to the destination's tax authority.

- Transactions where a seller fails to bill and collect the appropriate taxes even though he or she is authorized to do so.

  Mistakes do happen.

As always, buyers should watch for changes in tax laws, changes in reciprocal tax agreements, and related court decisions and rulings, as these may affect your personal purchases. In 2018, the United States Supreme Court handed down a decision on the case of *South Dakota v. Wayfair*, no. 17-494, which has caused states to enact laws regarding seller registration and the collection and remittance of sales taxes on sales completed in other states. Based on this ruling, state-level laws have been enacted that may read similar to this: "If an out-of-state seller is unregistered and makes at least one hundred thousand dollars in sales or more than two hundred thousand transactions in the state, then the seller must register and collect taxes from buyers and remit such to the tax authorities."

TAX COMPLIANCE

Usually, a noncommercial buyer does not think about whether each transaction is compliant with the tax laws. Most buyers trust that sellers are compliant with tax responsibilities, including billing for taxes when appropriate and remitting the appropriate tax amounts to tax authorities. However, sometimes a buyer should question the compliance level of the seller and consider any responsibilities they themselves may have to bear.

Buyers may be confident that most large-and medium-sized businesses, such as Walmart and Dell Computers, are compliant with tax laws. A large- or medium-sized company is usually more proactive in remaining compliant with the tax laws because they are more likely to be audited by different tax jurisdictions or monitored by consumer rights advocates.

Buyers may have less confidence that smaller businesses are compliant with tax laws. The smaller the business, the higher the chance it has neither the resources nor the experienced personnel to ensure compliance with its tax responsibilities.

Sometimes, noncommercial buyers do not bother to think about whether the seller is or is not in compliance with tax laws or whether the seller is making mistakes. In fact, most noncommercial buyers do not think at all about the taxes billed or whether they should be billed. However, a buyer should make it a regular practice to consider whether the seller has adhered to the tax requirements for the transaction. He or she may be billing the wrong amount(s).

If the seller demonstrates the ability to comply with tax requirements, then the buyer can relax a bit. However, if there are signs that the seller is not compliant, the user becomes responsible for ensuring that the appropriate taxes are billed and paid. If this does not happen, then the buyer needs to step up and remit any use taxes due. And if the seller is inappropriately billing taxes, for example, billing taxes on nontaxed items, and refuses to correct the mistake, then the buyer can report the seller to the relevant tax authority by using its tip line or website.

SUMMARY

Transactional taxes are imposed upon most goods and services that are procured by buyers for their own personal (noncommercial) use. These taxes have some similarities to the taxes imposed on commercial purchases. Every buyer should spend some time learning about these taxes and when they are applicable.

Buyers should also be aware some exemptions are available for personal purchases, similar to the exemptions available for commercial purchases. Every buyer should also spend time researching the exemptions so as to take advantage of them whenever possible.

Lastly, as with commercial taxes and exemptions, personal use taxes and exemptions are subject to change. Buyers should stay informed of any changes because their costs may be affected too.

Chapter 12

Summary

Transactional taxes are a part of our society. They are a necessity and cannot be avoided. With an understanding of taxes, taxpayers can prevent overpayment of taxes and avoid consequences from noncompliance, such as penalties and interest. However, it is up to the taxpayer to proactively learn about taxes and use his or her knowledge of taxes.

Different tiers of government have some differences in the tax laws they enact and how they enforce them. Taxes and tax rates may be modified when tax authorities see the need. They enact new legislation to keep up with commercial trends or meet political and/or financial needs. But the basic principle is similar: *to impose and collect taxes for the financing of the services provided*.

Not many buyers/consumers make an effort to stay informed of any changes to the tax laws. But businesses, which are more likely to be directly affected, usually have at least one employee who proactively monitors the tax landscape and shares information about any impactful changes.

Granted, not all transactional tax laws will impact every taxpayer. However, the tax laws that directly affect your business or personal transactions may make an impact on your costs, processes, and other responsibilities. Regardless, all buyers should stay informed of the different tax types, their scope, and any changes thereto.

Feel free to use all the exemptions applicable to your transactions, but be sure that your transaction qualifies and that you complete the appropriate forms and provide them to the seller in a timely manner.

Businesses should be aware of industry-specific tax responsibilities and exemptions. They should use this knowledge to minimize their tax costs and remain compliant.

All taxpayers are required to report taxes, remit taxes, and keep records related to their taxes. When a taxpayer is lax in attending to these responsibilities, he or she may be penalized with a fine or charged interest.

Many people fear tax audits, but if a taxpayer implements good tax policies and procedures to ensure compliance with tax laws, then his or her fear should lessen drastically.

It is important to handle transactional taxes properly in order to be compliant with tax law. The proper handling of taxes involves good policies, procedures, and business strategies, and the employment of adequately informed and well-trained personnel. An internal audit process should be formally defined and used to identify noncompliance. From the findings of audits and oversight, a manager can make timely adjustments to improve business procedures and minimize any negative impact on budgets, business plans, and contingency budgets.

A business should consider establishing a tax department and employing qualified personnel, who may have to be trained and provided with the resources and tools to proficiently carry out their duties. If not, employ help from tax service providers, tax consultants, and such to address tax responsibilities.

To maximize tax compliance, a business may need to formally identify its tax goals, which should be to maximize tax compliance and minimize tax costs. The steps to reaching these goals should be treated in a similar way as any other project plan with subgoals and subtasks, something that will become obvious when a tax department is setup and formal policies and procedures are in place.

Not many people take the time to consider transactional taxes and their impact on their own personal transactions. Most of the time, they see the tax listed on their receipts and do not question it. However, failure to ask questions may lead to underutilizing the exemptions available to them and are in effect paying taxes when they do not need to do so.

In general, taxpayers should not assume that tax accountants, tax attorneys, or other tax professionals understand transactional taxes. A smart strategy is to be informed enough to be able to identify and understand your tax costs, minimize the risk of an audit, and know when to hire a tax professional or consultant.

Important:

Do not wait for a tax auditor to identify any noncompliance with any tax law.

Remember:

Strive to maximize tax compliance, meanwhile efficiently and effectively addressing all your tax responsibilities and minimizing your tax costs.

Appendices

Supplemental Information

Appendix 1

Tax Exemption Certification Forms

The forms included in this appendix are to demonstrate and compare different form designs used for exemption declarations. Very brief notes are provided to share how the different forms may be used or to elaborate on the form's specific purpose.

Note: The forms included here may not be the latest versions.

Appendix number	State	Form number	Form title and comments
1.01	Texas	01-339	**Texas Sales and Use Tax Resale Certificate** This form is intended to declare an exemption from Texas-based taxes on a resale-based transaction. This is for items procured for the purpose of its resale, renting, and leasing in Texas. If this form is used, either a Texas sales tax permit number or other qualifying identification number will be needed.
1.02	Illinois	CRT-61	**Certificate of Resale** This form is to be used to declare a resale exemption in Illinois.
1.03	Hawaii	G-19	**Resale Certificate Special Form** Depending upon the taxpayer involved, this form may need to be used with the Hawaii tax form G-18.
1.04	Hawaii	G-17	**Resale Certificate for Goods— General Form 1** This form may be used to declare a resale exemption on a transaction made for resale.

Appendix number	State	Form number	Form title and comments
1.05	Hawaii	G-18	**Resale Certificate—General Form 2** This form is to be used with Hawaii tax form G-19 and is to provide supplemental information. Also, the purchases are for projects requiring a building permit.
1.06	Texas	01-339	**Texas Sales and Use Tax Exemption Certification** This form is intended to be used to take advantage of an exemption that is applicable to a non-resale-based transaction.
1.07	Texas	01-919	**Texas Direct Payment Exemption Certification Limited Sales, Excise, and Use Tax** This form will be used by an active direct payment permit holder to declare exemptions from taxable transactions and for which the permit holder will remit directly to the tax authority.
1.08	Illinois	ST-587	**Exemption Certificate(for Manufacturing, Production, Agriculture, and Coal and Aggregate Mining)** This form is made available for the specific industries listed on the title and purchases.
1.09	Illinois	EZ-1	**EZ-1 Building Materials Exemption Certificate** This exemption is for use with building materials that are procured for incorporation into a facility located in a designated zone or high-impact business. The buyer must apply and be approved in order to be able to use this form.

Appendix number	State	Form number	Form title and comments
1.10	Illinois	ST-589	**Certificate of Eligibility for Sales and Use Tax Exemption— Community Water Supply** This exemption applies to purchases related to the construction and maintenance of community water supply.
1.11	Texas	01-917	**Statement of Occasional Sale** A buyer may request a seller to provide this document to verify that the sale was an occasional sale.
1.12	Texas	01-907	**Texas Aircraft Exemption Certificate Out-of-State Registration and Use** This form is to be used when an aircraft is purchased in Texas but is to be registered and used outside Texas.
1.13	Texas	01-931	**Qualified Research Sales and Use Tax Exemption Certificate** This form is to be used when declaring an exemption on items based on qualifying research as described in Texas Code 151.3182.
1.14	Texas	01-929	**Exemption Certificate for Qualifying Data Centers or Qualifying Large Data Center Projects** This form is to be used to declare an exemption for purchases that qualify under the exemption for a qualified data center.
1.15	Louisiana	R-1399	**Antique Motor Vehicle Sales Tax Exemption Certificate** This form is to be used with the purchase of an antique motor vehicle that meets the defined criteria.

Appendix number	State	Form number	Form title and comments
1.16	Multijurisdiction		**Uniform Sales & Use Tax Certificate—Multijurisdiction** This multijurisdiction form may be used to declare exemption from sales taxes for the states listed on the form. Sellers and buyers are responsible for ensuring that the use of this form adheres to tax responsibilities of the listed states. This form consists of multiple pages.
1.17	Multistate	SSTGB FDD003	**Streamlined Sales Tax Agreement Certificate of Exemption** This form may be used by multiple states for the declaration of exemption from sales taxes. *Note:* Not all states recognize this as a valid form for declaring an exemption from sales taxes.
1.18	Arizona California New Mexico Texas	01-909-1	**Border States Uniform Sale for Resale Certificate** This form is to be used for transactions that involve a buyer and seller located in one of the four designated border states and a United Mexican State and the items procured are for the purpose of resale, lease, or rental.
1.19	Hawaii	G-61	**Export Exemption Certificate for General Excise and Liquor Taxes** This form is an export-related exemption form. Both the seller and buyer must complete this form. *Note:* Use taxes may apply for the destination jurisdiction.
1.20	Texas	01-374	**Texas Maquiladora Exemption Certificate—Limited Sales, Excise, and Use Tax** This form is to be used by buyers who are buying items from a Texas seller and will export the procured items to Mexico.

Appendix 1.01. Texas: Sales and Use Tax Resale Certificate

 01-339
(Rev.4-13/8)

Texas Sales and Use Tax Resale Certificate

Name of purchaser, firm or agency as shown on permit	Phone (Area code and number)

Address (Street & number, P.O. Box or Route number)

City, State, ZIP code

Texas Sales and Use Tax Permit Number *(must contain 11 digits)*

Out-of-state retailer's registration number or Federal Taxpayers Registry (RFC) number for retailers based in Mexico

(Retailers based in Mexico must also provide a copy of their Mexico registration form to the seller.)

I, the purchaser named above, claim the right to make a non-taxable purchase (for resale of the taxable items described below or on the attached order or invoice) from:

Seller: _____

Street address: _____

City, State, ZIP code: _____

Description of items to be purchased on the attached order or invoice:

_____
_____
_____

Description of the type of business activity generally engaged in or type of items normally sold by the purchaser:

_____
_____
_____

The taxable items described above, or on the attached order or invoice, will be resold, rented or leased by me within the geographical limits of the United States of America, its territories and possessions or within the geographical limits of the United Mexican States, in their present form or attached to other taxable items to be sold.

I understand that if I make any use of the items other than retention, demonstration or display while holding them for sale, lease or rental, I must pay sales tax on the items at the time of use based upon either the purchase price or the fair market rental value for the period of time used.

I understand that it is a criminal offense to give a resale certificate to the seller for taxable items that I know, at the time of purchase, are purchased for use rather than for the purpose of resale, lease or rental, and depending on the amount of tax evaded, the offense may range from a Class C misdemeanor to a felony of the second degree.

sign here ▶	Purchaser	Title	Date

This certificate should be furnished to the supplier.
Do not send the completed certificate to the Comptroller of Public Accounts.

Appendix 1.02. Illinois Certificate of Resale

 Illinois Department of Revenue

CRT-61 Certificate of Resale

Step 1: Identify the seller

1 Name _____

2 Business address _____

_____
City   State   Zip

Step 2: Identify the purchaser

3 Name _____

4 Business address _____

_____
City   State   Zip

5 Complete the information below. Check only one box.

☐ The purchaser is registered as a retailer with the Illinois
Department of Revenue. __ __ __ - __ __ __ __ .
                              Account ID number

☐ The purchaser is registered as a reseller with the Illinois
Department of Revenue. __ __ __ - __ __ __ __ .
                              Resale number

☐ The purchaser is authorized to do business out-of-state and
will resell and deliver property only to purchasers located
outside the state of Illinois. See Line 5 instructions.

Step 3: Describe the property

6 Describe the property that is being purchased for resale or
list the invoice number and the date of purchase.

_____

_____

_____

Step 4: Complete for blanket certificates

7 Complete the information below. Check only one box.

☐ I am the identified purchaser, and I certify that all of the
purchases that I make from this seller are for resale.

☐ I am the identified purchaser, and I certify that the following
percentage, _____ %, of all of the purchases that I make
from this seller are for resale.

Step 5: Purchaser's signature

I certify that I am purchasing the property described in Step 3
from the stated seller for the purpose of resale.

_____ __/__/____
Purchaser's signature   Date

**Note: It is the seller's responsibility to verify that the
purchaser's Illinois account ID or Illinois resale number is
valid and active. You can confirm this by visiting our web site
at tax.illinois.gov and using the Verify a Registered Business
tool.**

General information

When is a Certificate of Resale required?
Generally, a Certificate of Resale is required for proof that no tax
is due on any sale that is made tax-free as a sale for resale. The
purchaser, at the seller's request, must provide the information
that is needed to complete this certificate.

Who keeps the Certificate of Resale?
The seller must keep the certificate. We may request it as proof
that no tax was due on the sale of the specified property.
Do not mail the certificate to us.

Can other forms be used?
Yes. You can use other forms or statements in place of this
certificate but whatever you use as proof that a sale was made for
resale must contain
- the seller's name and address;
- the purchaser's name and address;
- a description of the property being purchased;
- a statement that the property is being purchased for resale;
- the purchaser's signature and date of signing; and
- either an Illinois account ID number, an Illinois resale number,
or a certification of resale to an out-of-state purchaser.

Note: A purchase order signed by the purchaser may be used
as a Certificate of Resale if it contains all of the above required
information.

CRT-61 (R-12/10)
IL-492-3850

When is a blanket certificate of resale used?
The purchaser may provide a blanket certificate of resale to
any seller from whom all purchases made are sales for resale.
A blanket certificate can also specify that a percentage of the
purchases made from the identified seller will be for resale. In
either instance, blanket certificates should be kept up-to-date.
If a specified percentage changes, a new certificate should be
provided. Otherwise, all certificates should be updated at least
every three years.

Specific instructions

Step 1: Identify the seller
Lines 1 and 2 Write the seller's name and mailing address.

Step 2: Identify the purchaser
Lines 3 and 4 Write the purchaser's name and mailing address.
Line 5 Check the statement that applies to the purchaser's
business, and provide any additional requested information.
Note: A statement by the purchaser that property will be sold for
resale will not be accepted by the department without supporting
evidence (e.g., proof of out-of-state registration).

Step 3: Describe the property
Line 6 On the lines provided, briefly describe the tangible
personal property that was purchased for resale or list the invoice
number and date of purchase.

Step 4: Complete for blanket certificates
Line 7 The purchaser must check the statement that applies,
and provide any additional requested information.

Step 5: Purchaser's signature
The purchaser must sign and date the form.

Appendix 1.03. Hawaii: Resale Certificate Special Form

FORM G-19
(REV. 2016)

STATE OF HAWAII — DEPARTMENT OF TAXATION

RESALE CERTIFICATE
SPECIAL FORM
(For use singly or with General Form 2)

To _____
Name of Seller

_____   _____
Address of Seller   Date of this Certificate

_____ _____ _____
City   State   Postal/ZIP Code

The undersigned hereby certifies the following under penalties set forth in section 231-36, Hawaii Revised Statutes (HRS), as Purchaser or as an authorized agent or representative of the named Purchaser, pursuant to section 237-13(2)(F), HRS, and Hawaii Administrative Rules (HAR), relating to resale certificates and sales at wholesale:

That the Purchaser is the holder of Hawaii Tax Identification No. GE __ __ __ - __ __ __ - __ __ __ __ - __ __ under the General Excise Tax Law and subject to the taxing jurisdiction of the State.

That the Purchaser is engaged in the contracting business or is subject to taxation the same as if so engaged.

That until this Certificate is revoked by notice in writing, it shall apply to all sales of materials or commodities which the Purchaser shall purchase from the Seller named above in connection with that certain work or project identified below, except those orders as to which the Purchaser shall specify by notice in writing that this Certificate does not apply. The work or project is:

_____
Brief description

_____
Location, described by street address

_____   _____
Tax Map Key Number   Building Permit Number

That all the materials and commodities to which this Certificate applies will be incorporated into the finished work or project identified above and will remain in such finished work or project in such form as to be perceptible to the senses.

That the work or project identified above is one in which the Purchaser is engaged as a part of his or her contracting business, or one which renders the Purchaser liable to the same tax as if engaged in the business of contracting, as set forth in section 237-4(a)(4), HRS, and section 18-237-4(a)(4), HAR, and that it is not a federal cost-plus contract governed by the election provided for by section 237-13(3)(C), HRS.

That the Purchaser, pursuant to section 237-13(2)(F)(i), HRS and section 18-237-13-02(d)(2)(B), HAR, shall pay to the seller the amount of any additional tax imposed upon the seller with respect to any transactions covered by this certificate.

_____   _____
Name of Purchaser   Signature

_____   _____
Address of Purchaser   Print Name of Signatory

_____ _____ _____   _____ _____
City   State   Postal/ZIP Code   Title (Owner, Partner or Member, Officer, or Duly Authorized Agent)   Date

Seller should retain this Certificate for Seller's files. Do NOT send to the Department of Taxation.

FORM G-19

Appendix 1.04. Hawaii: Resale Certificate for Goods—General Form 1

FORM G-17
(REV. 2016)

STATE OF HAWAII — DEPARTMENT OF TAXATION

RESALE CERTIFICATE FOR GOODS
GENERAL FORM 1
(PLEASE PRINT OR TYPE)

To _____
                    Name of Seller

_____   _____
        Address of Seller   Date of this Certificate

_____ _____ _____
   City   State   Postal/ZIP Code

The undersigned hereby certifies the following under the penalties set forth in section 231-36, Hawaii Revised Statutes (HRS), as Purchaser or as an authorized agent or representative of the named Purchaser:

That the Purchaser is the holder of Hawaii Tax Identification No. **GE** __ __ __ - __ __ __ - __ __ __ __ - __ __ under the General Excise Tax Law and subject to the taxing jurisdiction of the State.

That the nature and character of the Purchaser's business is:

_____

_____

_____

_____

That this Certificate, until revoked by notice in writing, shall apply to all purchases of tangible personal property which the Purchaser shall purchase from the Seller named above except those orders which the Purchaser specifies by notice in writing that this Certificate does not apply.

That all of the purchases of tangible personal property to which this Certificate applies:

☐ are purchases for resale at retail or leases under Chapter 237, HRS; **and/or**

☐ are purchases for resale at wholesale under Chapter 237, HRS;

That the Purchaser, pursuant to section 237-13(2)(F)(i), HRS, and section 18-237-13-02(d)(2)(B), Hawaii Administrative Rules, shall pay to the seller the amount of any additional tax imposed upon the seller with respect to any transactions covered by this certificate.

_____   _____
        Name of Purchaser   Signature

_____   _____
        Address of Purchaser   Print Name of Signatory

_____ _____ _____   _____ _____
   City   State   Postal/ZIP Code   Title (Owner, Partner or Member, Officer, or Duly Authorized Agent)   Date

Seller should retain this Certificate for Seller's files. Do NOT send to the Department of Taxation.

FORM G-17

Appendix 1.05. Hawaii: Resale Certificate—General Form 2

FORM G-18
(REV. 2016)

STATE OF HAWAII — DEPARTMENT OF TAXATION

RESALE CERTIFICATE
GENERAL FORM 2

(For use where the Purchaser is to give Certificate in Special Form when
making purchases for projects where a building permit is required.)

To _____
Name of Seller

_____   _____
Address of Seller   Date of this Certificate

_____ _____ _____
City   State   Postal/ZIP Code

The undersigned hereby certifies the following under the penalties set forth in section 231-36, Hawaii Revised Statutes (HRS), as Purchaser or as an authorized agent or representative of the named Purchaser, pursuant to section 237-13(2)(F), HRS, and Hawaii Administrative Rules (HAR), relating to resale certificates and sales at wholesale:

That the Purchaser is the holder of Hawaii Tax Identification No. GE __ __ __ -__ __ __ -__ __ __ __ -__ __ under the General Excise Tax Law and subject to the taxing jurisdiction of the State.

That the nature and character of the Purchaser's business is:

_____

_____

That until this Certificate is revoked by notice in writing it shall apply to all sales of tangible personal property which the Purchaser shall purchase from the Seller named above, except those orders as to which the Purchaser shall specify by notice in writing that this Certificate does not apply.

That all of the tangible personal property to which this Certificate applies will be used for purposes of resale, as set forth in section 237-4(a)(1), HRS, and section 18-237-4(a)(1), HAR; or for incorporation by the Purchaser into a manufactured product which will be sold, as set forth in section 237-4(a)(2), HRS, and section 18-237-4(a)(2), HAR; or for incorporation by the Purchaser (who is engaged in the contracting business or is subject to taxation the same as if engaged in the business of contracting) into a structure or other improvement on land as set forth in section 237-4(a)(4), HRS, and section 18-237-4(a)(4), HAR.

That when materials or commodities are purchased for incorporation into a structure or other improvement on land for which a building permit is required, the Purchaser will give notice in writing to the Seller as to this project, and those purchases shall be covered by a Special Form of resale certificate for each project. However, the Special Form shall not be required for purchases made for addition to general stock.

That the Purchaser, pursuant to section 237-13(2)(F)(i), HRS, and section 18-237-13-02(d)(2)(B), HAR, shall pay to the seller the amount of any additional tax imposed upon the seller with respect to any transactions covered by this certificate.

_____   _____
Name of Purchaser   Signature

_____   _____
Address of Purchaser   Print Name of Signatory

_____ _____ _____   _____   _____
City   State   Postal/ZIP Code   Title (Owner, Partner or Member, Officer, or Duly Authorized Agent)   Date

Seller should retain this Certificate for Seller's files. Do NOT send to the Department of Taxation.

FORM G-18

Appendix 1.06. Texas: Sales and Use Tax Exemption Certification

 01-339 (Back)
(Rev.4-13/8)

Texas Sales and Use Tax Exemption Certification
This certificate does not require a number to be valid.

Name of purchaser, firm or agency	
Address (Street & number, P.O. Box or Route number)	Phone (Area code and number)
City, State, ZIP code	

I, the purchaser named above, claim an exemption from payment of sales and use taxes (for the purchase of taxable items described below or on the attached order or invoice) from:

Seller: _____

Street address: _____ City, State, ZIP code: _____

Description of items to be purchased or on the attached order or invoice:

_____

_____

_____

_____

Purchaser claims this exemption for the following reason:

_____

_____

_____

_____

I understand that I will be liable for payment of all state and local sales or use taxes which may become due for failure to comply with the provisions of the Tax Code and/or all applicable law.

I understand that it is a criminal offense to give an exemption certificate to the seller for taxable items that I know, at the time of purchase, will be used in a manner other than that expressed in this certificate, and depending on the amount of tax evaded, the offense may range from a Class C misdemeanor to a felony of the second degree.

sign here ▶	Purchaser	Title	Date

NOTE: This certificate cannot be issued for the purchase, lease, or rental of a motor vehicle.

THIS CERTIFICATE DOES NOT REQUIRE A NUMBER TO BE VALID.

Sales and Use Tax "Exemption Numbers" or "Tax Exempt" Numbers do not exist.

This certificate should be furnished to the supplier.
Do not send the completed certificate to the Comptroller of Public Accounts.

Appendix 1.07. Texas: Direct Payment Exemption Certification— Limited Sales, Excise, and Use Tax

 01-919
(7-05)

STATE OF TEXAS

TEXAS DIRECT PAYMENT EXEMPTION CERTIFICATION
LIMITED SALES, EXCISE AND USE TAX

Direct payment permit number

Name of purchaser, firm or agency

Address (Street & number, P.O. Box or Route number)

Phone (Area code and number)

City, State, ZIP code

I, the undersigned, hereby claim an exemption from payment of state, city, county, special purpose district, and transit authority/department sales and use taxes upon purchase of taxable items from:

Seller: _____

Street address: _____ City, State, ZIP code: _____

Description of items to be purchased (If this space is left blank, this certificate covers everything on the attached order, invoice, or billing):

_____

_____

_____

_____

_____

_____

This certificate does not cover:

    (1) Purchases of taxable items to be resold;

    (2) Sales or rentals to any purchaser other than the permit holder;

    (3) Sales or rentals of motor vehicles subject to the motor vehicle sales and use tax (Chapter 152);

    (4) Materials or supplies used, transferred, or consumed by a provider of a nontaxable service selling the service to a direct payment permit holder.

This certificate is not valid for lump-sum new construction projects to improve real property for a direct payment permit holder.

The permit holder agrees not to permit others (including its contractors and repairmen) to use the undersigned's direct payment authorization to purchase materials tax-free.

The undersigned agrees to accrue and pay the tax to the Comptroller of Public Accounts as required by statute.

sign here ▶ Authorized signature | Permit holder | Date

This certificate should be furnished to the supplier. Do **not** send the completed certificate to the Comptroller of Public Accounts.

Appendix 1.08. Illinois: Exemption Certificate (for Manufacturing, Production, Agriculture, and Coal and Aggregate Mining)

Illinois Department of Revenue

ST-587 Exemption Certificate (for Manufacturing, Production Agriculture, and Coal and Aggregate Mining)

Step 1: Identify the seller
The seller must keep this certificate.

Name _____   Address _____
                                          Number and street

Phone (____) _____   _____
                                   City   State   ZIP

Step 2: Identify the purchaser (lessor)

Name _____   Phone (____) _____

Address _____   Date of purchase ___/___/___
        Number and street   Month Day Year

City _____ State ____ ZIP ____   Write the purchaser's Illinois account ID number, FEIN or SSN.

Illinois account ID number _____

FEIN _____ SSN _____

Step 3: Identify the lessee

Name _____   Address _____
                                          Number and street

Phone (____) _____   _____
                                   City   State   ZIP

Step 4: Identify the item(s) you are purchasing (or leasing)

Type of item(s) _____
Serial number(s) _____

Step 5: Identify how you will use the item(s) listed in Step 4. Check the appropriate box. You must complete this step and also Step 6 if you are submitting this form as a blanket certificate.

I state that this item will be used

☐ primarily in the manufacturing or assembling of tangible personal property for wholesale or retail sale or lease, including graphic arts production.
☐ primarily in production agriculture.
☐ primarily for coal and aggregate exploration and related mining, off-highway hauling, processing, maintenance, and reclamation, but excluding motor vehicles required to be registered under the Illinois Vehicle Code.

Step 6: Blanket Certificate Complete this step only if you are using this form as a blanket certificate. Check the appropriate box.
I am the identified purchaser, and I certify that

☐ all of the purchases that I make from this seller are eligible for the exemption identified in Step 5.
☐ the following percentage, _____ %, of all of the purchases that I make from this seller are eligible for the exemption identified in Step 5.

Step 7: Sign below

Under penalties of perjury, I state that I have examined this certificate and, to the best of my knowledge, it is true, correct, and complete.

_____   ___/___/___
Purchaser's signature   Date

You may photocopy this form or you may obtain additional forms by visiting our website at **tax.illinois.gov**.

ST-587 (R-12/19)   This form is authorized as outlined under the tax or fee Act imposing the tax or fee for which this form is filed. Disclosure of this information is required. Failure to provide information may result in this form not being processed and may result in a penalty.

Appendix 1.09. Illinois: EZ-1 Building Materials Exemption Certificate

 Illinois Department of Revenue

EZ-1 Certificate of Exempt Purchase for Building Materials
Use of this form requires the purchaser to have a valid Building Materials Exemption Certificate from the Illinois Department of Revenue.

Step 1:   Identify the seller

The seller must keep this certificate.

Name _____   Address _____
                                                    Number and street

Phone (_____)_____   _____
                                                    City   State   ZIP

Step 2:   Identify the purchaser and purchaser's certificate number

Name _____   Phone (_____)_____

Address _____   Date of purchase ____/____/____
        Number and street   Month   Day   Year

City _____ State _____ ZIP _____   Building materials exemption certificate number of the purchaser:

                                              _____

Step 3:   Location or address of the real estate into which building materials will be permanently incorporated

Name of Zone or High Impact Business _____

Project Name _____

Location _____   Address _____
                                                    Number and street
_____   _____
                                    OR   City   State   ZIP

Step 4:   Identify the building materials you are purchasing

Description of building materials purchased _____

_____

_____

_____

_____

_____

Step 5:   Sign below

I certify that the building materials described above will be permanently incorporated into real estate in the location indicated above as rehabilitation, renovation, and/or new construction for this project.

                                              ____/____/____
_____   Date
Purchaser's signature

For more information about Building Materials Exemptions, visit the Business Incentives Reporting and Building Materials Exemption Certification web page at **https://www2.illinois.gov/rev/businesses/incentives/Pages/default.aspx.**

Note to seller: It is the seller's responsibility to verify that the purchaser's building materials exemption certificate number is valid and active. You can confirm this by using the "Verify the validity of a Building Material Exemption Certificate" tool on our website at **tax.illinois.gov.**

EZ-1 (R-12/21) | This form is authorized by the Illinois Retailers' Occupation Tax Act. Disclosure of this information is required.
Printed by the authority of the State of Illinois | Failure to provide information may result in this form not being processed and may result in a penalty.
one copy, electronic only

Appendix 1.10. Illinois: Certificate of Eligibility for Sales and Use Tax Exemption—Community Water Supply

 Illinois Department of Revenue

ST-589 Certificate of Eligibility for Sales and Use Tax Exemption — Community Water Supply

The seller must keep this certificate. The community water supply must always complete Steps 1 through 4. If the purchaser is a contractor, the contractor also must complete Step 5.

Step 1: Identify the seller

Name _____

Phone (____) _____

Address _____
Number and street

City _____ State ___ ZIP ___

Step 2: Identify the community water supply

Name _____

Address _____
Number and street

City _____ State _____ ZIP _____

Phone (____) _____

Date of purchase ___ / ___ / ___
Month   Day   Year

Illinois EPA Water Supply Facility Number:

IL ___ ___ ___ ___ ___ ___ ___

FEIN ___ ___ - ___ ___ ___ ___ ___ ___ ___

Step 3: Identify the tangible personal property you are purchasing

Description of tangible personal property _____

Vehicle identification number (VIN) or other identifying number for items that must be titled or registered with an agency of Illinois state government _____

Step 4: Identify how the tangible personal property will be used and sign below

This is a purchase by the community water supply identified above, and (check one)

☐ this tangible personal property is being purchased and used in the construction or maintenance of structures and physical plant owned by the community water supply and will be physically incorporated into the structures and physical plant; or

☐ this tangible personal property will not be physically incorporated into the structures and physical plant owned by a community water supply but is being purchased for use in the construction or maintenance of a community water supply. **Note:** This exempt purpose can be claimed only when the purchaser is the community water supply, _not_ a contractor.

Sign here

Under penalties of perjury, I state that I have examined this certificate and to the best of my knowledge it is true, correct, and complete. I further state that the above-identified community water supply meets all the requirements of Section 2-5(39) of the Retailers' Occupation Tax Act and that the not-for-profit corporation is in good standing and has not been dissolved. If the not-for-profit corporation is a foreign not-for-profit corporation, I also state that it has obtained a certificate of authority to conduct affairs in Illinois and that the certificate has not been withdrawn.

_____ ___ / ___ / ___
Signature of chief executive officer or duly authorized designee   Date

Step 5: If the purchaser is a contractor, also complete the following and sign below

Contractor's Name _____

Phone (____) _____

Address _____
Number and street

City _____ State _____ ZIP _____

I am a contractor and the tangible personal property I am purchasing will be physically incorporated into the structures and physical plant owned by a community water supply in fulfillment of a construction contract with a not-for-profit corporation that operates the community water supply and is eligible for this exemption. Under penalties of perjury, I state that I have examined this certificate and, to the best of my knowledge, it is true, correct, and complete.

_____ ___ / ___ / ___
Contractor's signature   Date

If you have questions about the community water supply sales and use tax exemption, call the Illinois Department of Revenue at **(217) 785-6606**. Additional forms are available on our website at **tax.illinois.gov**.

ST-589 (N-10/15)

This form is authorized as outlined under the tax or fee Act imposing the tax or fee for which this form is filed. Disclosure of this information is required. Failure to provide information may result in this form not being processed and may result in a penalty.

Appendix 1.11. Texas: Statement of Occasional Sale

 01-917
(Rev.3-06/2)

STATEMENT OF OCCASIONAL SALE

Entity name (Corporation, partnership or sole proprietorship)		
Mailing address		
City	State	ZIP code
Daytime phone (Area code and number)	Provide a brief description of your business activities	

I have read the State of Texas, Comptroller of Public Accounts, Limited Sales and Use Tax Rule 3.316 regarding Occasional Sales (34 Texas Administrative Code §3.316), and I hereby acknowledge that the following sale I made qualifies as an occasional sale:

Description of item sold (include year, model, serial numbers, etc.):

_____

_____

_____

Date item sold	Sales price of item
Item sold to: *(Name)*	
Address	

Check the box below that applies to you:

☐ This was a transfer without change in ownership. My percentage of ownership prior to transfer was _____ %; my percentage of ownership after transfer was _____ %.

☐ I certify that I do not hold a sales tax permit in Texas or any other state and I have not made a sale of more than one other taxable item within the previous twelve months.

☐ I certify that I sold the entire operating assets of (1) a whole business or (2) a separate division, branch, or identifiable segment of a business with attributable income and expenses that can be separately established from the books of account or records of the business.

I understand that if any information provided here is later found to be incorrect, I may be held liable for collection of sales or use tax on the above item.

Print name	Title
sign here ▶ Signature	Date

You have certain rights under Chapters 552 and 559, Government Code, to review, request, and correct information we have on file about you. For more information contact the Texas State Comptroller's office.

Appendix 1.12. Texas: Aircraft Exemption Certificate—Out-of-State Registration and Use

 01-907
(Rev.12-01/3)

TEXAS AIRCRAFT EXEMPTION CERTIFICATE
OUT-OF-STATE REGISTRATION AND USE

Under Ch. 559, Government Code, you are entitled to review, request, and correct information we have on file about you, with limited exceptions in accordance with Ch. 552, Government Code. To request information for review or to request error correction, contact us at the address or toll-free number listed on this form.

Name of purchaser

Address (Street & number and P.O. Box number)   Phone (Area code & number)

City, State, ZIP code

Name of seller   Seller's Texas sales tax permit number

Address (Street & number and P.O. Box number)   Phone (Area code & number)

City, State, ZIP code

The undersigned hereby certifies that the aircraft described below was purchased on _____

Date of sale

for a total sales price of $ _____ of which $ _____ was allowed as a trade-in,

resulting in a net sales price of $ _____ .

Aircraft make	Model	Serial number	FAA registration number (Tail number)

The aircraft will be registered in _____ , _____ as recorded with Federal Aviation Administration.

City   State

The aircraft will be **hangared** in _____ , _____ and is not purchased for use in Texas.

City   State

My correct mailing and location address are _____

Mailing address

_____

Location address

I claim an exemption from the Texas sales tax pursuant to Texas Tax Code Section 151.328(a)(4) because the aircraft is purchased for registration and use outside Texas.

I understand that by signing this form, I am authorizing the Texas Comptroller of Public Accounts to furnish copies to officials of my home state. I understand that the purpose of providing this information to officials of my home state is to facilitate the enforcement of any taxes imposed on the purchase or use of the aircraft in my home state.

I understand that it is a misdemeanor punishable by a fine not to exceed $500 to provide this certificate of exemption if I know the aircraft will be used in a manner other than for registration and use outside Texas.

sign here► Purchaser's signature   Date

sign here► Seller's signature   Date

(Original to be retained by seller, seller to send copy to the Texas Comptroller of Public Accounts, Business Activity Research Team, P.O. Box 13003, Austin, Texas, 78711-3003, and copy to the Purchaser.)

Appendix 1.13. Texas: Qualified Research Sales and Use Tax Exemption Certificate

 01-931
(Rev.2-17/2)

Qualified Research Sales and Use Tax Exemption Certificate

Persons engaged in qualified research who hold a registration number issued by the Comptroller must provide this completed form to sellers when claiming an exemption from Texas sales and use tax on items that qualify for exemption under Texas Tax Code Section 151.3182. The certificate may serve as a blanket exemption certificate covering all qualifying purchases.

This form may not be used to claim exemption from tax on motor vehicles, including trailers.

Seller Information
Name
Address *(Street and number, P.O. Box or route number)*
City, State, ZIP code — Phone *(Area code and number)*

Purchaser Information
Name — Qualified Research registration number: R D
Address *(Street and number, P.O. Box or route number)*
City, State, ZIP code — Phone *(Area code and number)*

I, the purchaser named above, claim an exemption from payment of sales and use taxes for the following items:

Description of items to be purchased or on the attached order or invoice

_____

_____

_____

_____

_____

_____

I understand that I will be liable for payment of all state and local sales or use taxes which may become due for failure to comply with the provisions of the Tax Code and/or applicable law.

I understand that it is a criminal offense to issue an exemption certificate to the seller for taxable items that I know, at the time of purchase, will be used in a manner that does not qualify for the exemptions found in Tax Code Section 151.3182, and depending on the amount of tax evaded, the offense may range from a Class C misdemeanor to a felony of the second degree.

| sign here ▶ | Authorized Purchaser's signature | Purchaser's name *(Print or type)* | Date |

This certificate should be furnished to the supplier.
*Do **not** send the completed certificate to the Comptroller of Public Accounts.*

Appendix 1.14. Texas: Exemption Certificate for Qualifying Data Centers or Qualifying Large Data Center Projects

 01-929
(Rev.2-17/3)

Exemption Certificate for Qualifying Data Centers or Qualifying Large Data Center Projects

This form must be provided by a qualifying occupant, owner or operator to a seller for the purchase of items that qualify for exemption from Texas state sales and use tax under Texas Tax Code Section 151.359 or Texas state and local sales and use tax under Tax Code Section 151.3595. (See a list of qualifying and non-qualifying items on the back of this form.)

Check one: ☐ This exemption certificate is claimed for state sales and use tax only for qualifying data centers subject to Tax Code Section 151.359.

☐ This exemption is claimed for both state and local sales and use tax for qualifying large data center projects subject to Tax Code Section 151.3595.

Seller Information
Name
Address *(Street and number, P.O. Box or route number)*
City, State, ZIP code   Phone *(Area code and number)*

Purchaser Information
Qualifying Data Center name   Qualifying Data Center registration number
Qualifying Occupant, Owner or Operator name   Qualifying Occupant, Owner or Operator registration number
Qualifying Occupant, Owner or Operator address *(Street and number, P.O. Box or route number)*   Check one ☐ Occupant ☐ Owner ☐ Operator
City, State, ZIP code   Phone *(Area code and number)*

I, the purchaser named above, claim an exemption from payment of sales and use taxes for the following items:

Description of items to be purchased or on the attached order or invoice

_____

_____

_____

_____

_____

_____

I understand that I will be liable for payment of all state and local sales or use taxes which may become due for failure to comply with the provisions of the Tax Code and/or applicable law.

I understand that it is a criminal offense to give an exemption certificate to the seller for taxable items that I know, at the time of purchase, will be used in a manner other than that expressed in this certificate, and depending on the amount of tax evaded, the offense may range from a Class C misdemeanor to a felony of the second degree.

sign here ▶	Authorized Purchaser's signature	Purchaser's name *(Print or type)*	Date

This certificate should be furnished to the seller.
*Do **not** send the completed certificate to the Comptroller of Public Accounts.*

Appendix 1.15. Louisiana: Antique Motor Vehicle Sales Tax Exemption Certificate

R-1399 (7/19)

LA R.S.47:6040 provides a sales tax exemption to antique motor vehicles which meet the following criteria:

- The motor vehicle was manufactured at least twenty-five years ago and is not used for commercial purposes; and
- The motor vehicle is valued in excess of ten thousand dollars.
- Registration and licensing of the motor vehicle is subject to the payment of fees for a license plate for an antique motor vehicle as provided in LA R.S. 47:463.8(B).
- Applicable to sales on or after July 1, 2019.

PLEASE PRINT OR TYPE

Purchaser Information			
Name			
Address			
City		State	ZIP

Antique Motor Vehicle Information		
Make	Model	Year
Vehicle Identification Number (VIN)	Purchase Date of Vehicle *(mm/dd/yyyy)*	Sales Price of Vehicle

Under penalty of perjury, I declare that I have examined this form and accompanying documents, and to the best of my knowledge and belief, it is true, correct, and complete. Declaration of preparer (other than taxpayer) is based on all information of which preparer has knowledge.

Certification of Purchaser		
Name	Signature	Date *(mm/dd/yyyy)*

Questions about the completion of this form should be sent to Sales.Inquiries@l.gov.

213

Appendix 1.16. Uniform Sales and Use Tax Certificate— Multijurisdiction

UNIFORM SALES & USE TAX RESALE CERTIFICATE — MULTIJURISDICTION

The below-listed states have indicated that this certificate is acceptable as a resale/exemption certificate for sales/use tax, subject to the instructions and notes on pages 2—6. The issuing Buyer and the recipient Seller have the responsibility to determine the proper use of this certificate under applicable laws in each state, as these may change from time to time. This form was revised as of December 9, 2020.

Issued to Seller: _____

Address: _____

I certify that: is engaged or is registered as a
Name of Firm (Buyer): _____   ☐ Wholesaler
Address: _____   ☐ Retailer
_____   ☐ Manufacturer
_____   ☐ Seller
_____   ☐ Lessor (see notes on pages 2—4)
_____   ☐ Other (Specify) _____

and is registered for sales/use tax with the below-listed states and cities within which Seller would deliver purchases to Buyer and that any such purchases are for wholesale, resale, or ingredients or components of a new product or service to be resold, leased, or rented in the normal course of business. Buyer is in the business of wholesaling, retailing, manufacturing, leasing (renting), or selling the following:

Description of Business: _____

General description of tangible property or taxable services to be purchased from the Seller: _____

State	State Registration, Seller's Permit, or ID Number of Purchaser	State	State Registration, Seller's Permit, or ID Number of Purchaser
AL[1]		NE	
AR		NJ	
AZ[2]		NM[4,19]	
CA[3]		NC[20]	
CO[4,5]		ND	
CT[6]		OH[21]	
FL[7]		OK[22]	
GA[8]		PA[23]	
HI[4,9]		RI[24]	
ID[10]		SC	
IL[4,11]		SD[25]	
IA		TN[26]	
KS[12]		TX[27]	
KY[13]		UT	
ME[14]		VT[28]	
MD[15]		WA[29]	
MI[16]		WI[30]	
MN[17]			
MO[18]			

I further certify that if any property or service so purchased tax-free is used or consumed by Buyer so as to make it subject to sales/use tax, Buyer will pay the tax due directly to the proper taxing authority when state law so provides or inform the Seller for added tax billing. This certificate shall be a part of each order that Buyer may hereafter give to Seller, unless otherwise specified, and shall be valid until canceled by Buyer in writing or revoked by the city or state.

Under penalties of perjury, I swear or affirm that the information on this form is true and correct as to every material matter.

Authorized Signature: _____
                        (Owner, Partner, or Corporate Officer, or other authorized signer of Buyer)

Title: _____
Date: _____

1

Appendix 1.17. Multistate: Streamlined Sales Tax Agreement Certificate of Exemption

Streamlined Sales Tax Certificate of Exemption

Streamlined Sales Tax Governing Board, Inc.

Do not send this form to the Streamlined Sales Tax Governing Board.
Send the completed form to the seller and keep a copy for your records.

This is a multi-state form for use in the states listed. Not all states allow all exemptions listed on this form. The purchaser is responsible for ensuring it is eligible for the exemption in the state it is claiming the tax exemption from. Check with the state for exemption information and requirements. The purchaser is liable for any tax and interest, and possible civil and criminal penalties imposed by the state, if the purchaser is not eligible to claim this exemption.

1. ☐ Check if this certificate is for a single purchase. Enter the related invoice/purchase order # _____

2. A. Purchaser's name _____

Print or type

B. Business address _____ City _____ State ____ Country ____ Zip code ____

C. Name of seller from whom you are purchasing, leasing or renting _____

D. Seller's address _____ City _____ State ____ Country ____ Zip code ____

3. **Purchaser's type of business.** Check the number that best describes your business.

☐ 01 Accommodation and food services
☐ 02 Agriculture, forestry, fishing, hunting
☐ 03 Construction
☐ 04 Finance and insurance
☐ 05 Information, publishing and communications
☐ 06 Manufacturing
☐ 07 Mining

☐ 08 Real estate
☐ 09 Rental and leasing
☐ 10 Retail trade
☐ 11 Transportation and warehousing
☐ 12 Utilities
☐ 13 Wholesale trade
☐ 14 Business services

☐ 15 Professional services
☐ 16 Education and health-care services
☐ 17 Nonprofit organization
☐ 18 Government
☐ 19 Not a business
☐ 20 Other (*explain*)

4. **Reason for exemption.** Check the letter that identifies the reason for the exemption.

☐ A Federal government (*Department*) * _____
☐ B State or local government (*Name*) * _____
☐ C Tribal government (*Name*) * _____
☐ D Foreign diplomat # _____
☐ E Charitable organization *
☐ F Religious organization *
☐ G Resale *
* see Instructions on back (page 2)

☐ H Agricultural Production *
☐ I Industrial production/manufacturing *
☐ J Direct pay permit *
☐ K Direct Mail *
☐ L Other (*Explain*) _____
☐ M Educational Organization *

5. **Identification (ID) number:** Enter the ID number as required in the instructions for each state in which you are claiming an exemption. If claiming multiple exemption reasons, enter the letters identifying each reason as listed in Section 4 for each state.

	ID number	State/Country Reason		ID number	State/Country Reason
AR			NV		
GA			OH		
IA			OK		
IN			RI		
KS			SD		
KY			TN		
MI			UT		
MN			VT		
NC			WA		
ND			WI		
NE			WV		
NJ			WY		

6. I declare that the information on this certificate is correct and complete to the best of my knowledge and belief.

Signature of authorized purchaser _____ Print name _____ Title _____ Date _____

SSTGB Form F0003 Exemption Certificate (Revised 12/21/2021)

Appendix 1.18. Arizona, California, New Mexico, Texas: Border States Uniform Sale for Resale Certificate

 01-909-1
(10-95)

BORDER STATES
UNIFORM SALE FOR RESALE CERTIFICATE
Accepted in Arizona, California, New Mexico and Texas

This certificate is to be completed by the purchaser and furnished to the vendor who shall retain it. Incomplete certificates must not be accepted in good faith.

SELLER INFORMATION

Seller: _____

Street Address: _____

City, State, Country, ZIP code: _____

PURCHASER INFORMATION

1 Purchaser: _____

Street Address: _____

City, State, Country, ZIP code: _____

2 I am engaged in the business of: _____

3 The property is purchased for resale, and will be resold in the state(s) or country noted below for which I have valid business tax permit(s):

Permit/Identification Number

a State   _____   _____

b State   _____   _____

c Country   United States   _____

d Country   United Mexican States   _____

4 Description of the property being purchased _____
_____
_____
_____

5 Check Applicable Box: ☐ Single Purchase Certificate   ☐ Blanket Certificate

CERTIFICATION

I understand that if I make any use of the item other than retention, demonstration, or display while holding it for sale in the regular course of business, I must pay use tax in that state or country measured by the purchase price of such property or other authorized amount. I further understand it may be a criminal offense to give a seller a resale certificate for a taxable item which I know, at the time of purchase, is purchased for use rather than for the purpose of resale, lease or rental. I certify that these purchases are exempt per the appropriate laws of the state or country of purchase and that the information on this certificate is true, accurate and complete.

Signature of Purchaser _____ **Date** _____

Title _____

Appendix 1.19. Hawaii: Export Exemption Certificate for General Excise and Liquor Taxes

FORM G-61
(REV. 2019)

STATE OF HAWAII — DEPARTMENT OF TAXATION
EXPORT EXEMPTION CERTIFICATE
FOR GENERAL EXCISE AND LIQUOR TAXES

PART I — Information About the Manufacturer, Producer, Contractor, Service Provider, or Seller

Name | Type of Organization (e.g., Corporation, Partnership, Individual, etc.)

Address (number and street) | City, State, and Postal/ZIP Code

Hawaii Tax I.D. Number
GE __ __ __ - __ __ __ __ - __ __ __ __ - __ __ | Liquor Permit Number (if applicable)

Description of the manufacturer, producer, contractor, service provider, or seller's business

PART II — Information About the Purchaser, Consumer, or User

Name | Type of Organization (e.g., Corporation, Partnership, Individual, etc.)

Address (number and street) | City, State, and Postal/ZIP Code

PART III — Tangible Personal Property/Intangible/Contracting/Services/Liquor Included in Transaction

A. **Description** of tangible personal property/intangible/contracting/services/liquor

B. **Value** of tangible personal property/intangible/contracting/services/liquor or gross proceeds involved

CERTIFICATION BY MANUFACTURER, PRODUCER, CONTRACTOR, SERVICE PROVIDER, OR SELLER AND PURCHASER, CONSUMER, OR USER

The undersigned manufacturer, producer, contractor, service provider, or seller (provider); and purchaser, consumer, or user hereby certify, pursuant to sections 231-36, 237-29.5, 237-29.53, 237-29.57 or 244D-4.3, Hawaii Revised Statutes (HRS), relating to export exemption and certification:

   (1) that the information provided in Parts I, II, and III above are true and correct; and

   (2) that until this certificate is revoked by notice in writing by either of the parties who signed the certificate or the Department of Taxation, it shall apply to this order or contract of sale between the manufacturer, producer, contractor, service provider, or seller; and the purchaser, consumer, or user.

The provider certifies that he or she will remit the tax due on the sale of the tangible personal property/intangible/contracting/services/liquor, as imposed by Chapters 237 and 244D, HRS, to the Department of Taxation if:

   (1) the place of delivery of the property, intangible or liquor for which the export exemption was claimed is not outside the State;

   (2) the property, intangible or liquor was not shipped or transmitted by the provider to the purchaser at a place of delivery outside the State; or

   (3) the intangible, contracting or services was not resold, consumed, or used outside the State.

Manufacturer, producer, contractor, service provider, or seller signature | Purchaser, consumer, or user signature

Print name of signatory | Print name of signatory

Title | Date | Title | Date

Provider should retain this certificate for the provider's files. DO NOT send to the Department of Taxation.

FORM G-61

Appendix 1.20. Texas: Maquiladora Exemption Certificate—Limited Sales, Excise, and Use Tax

01-374
(Rev.5-09/2)

TEXAS MAQUILADORA EXEMPTION CERTIFICATE –
LIMITED SALES, EXCISE AND USE TAX

Maquiladora exemption permit number

Name of purchaser

Street address

City, state, ZIP Code

The undersigned hereby claims exemption from the payment of state and local taxes on its purchases of taxable items for export to Mexico from:

Seller: _____

Street address: _____

City, state, ZIP Code: _____

This certificate will remain in effect until the seller is otherwise notified and does not cover purchases of taxable items to be resold in the form in which they are purchased.

The undersigned agrees to accrue and pay tax to the Texas Comptroller of Public Accounts on any goods purchased under this certificate that are not exported to Mexico prior to their use.

This certificate is not valid unless accompanied by a copy of the Maquiladora Export Permit issued by the Texas Comptroller of Public Accounts.

Name of permit holder *(Type or print)*	sign here ▶ Authorized signature	Date

Appendix 2

Application Forms for Tax Exemption

The forms included here are to demonstrate and compare the different designs of the application forms that must be completed for specific exemptions.

Note: The forms included may not be the latest versions.

Appendix number	State	Form number	Form title and comments
2.01	Oklahoma	13-16-A	Application for Sales Tax Exemption
2.02	Oklahoma	13-88	Application for Sales Tax Exemption by Motion Picture or Television Production Companies
2.03	Oklahoma	13-55	Application for 100% Disabled Veteran Household Member Exemption Card
2.04	Oklahoma	13-55-A	Application for Surviving Spouse of a 100% Disabled Veteran Household Member Exemption Card
2.05	Oklahoma	13-36	Application for Sales/Use Tax Exemption for Volunteer Fire Departments
2.06	New Mexico	ACD-31050	Application for Nontaxable Transaction Certificates

Appendix 2.01. Oklahoma: Application for Sales Tax Exemption

Form 13-16-A
Revised 11-2021

Oklahoma Tax Commission
Application for Sales Tax Exemption

1. Federal Employer Identification Number	2. Is Organization Incorporated? ☐ Yes ☐ No
3. Legal Name of Organization:	4. Business Phone Number:

5. Organization Physical Location (street and number or directions. Do NOT use post office box or rural route number):

6. City:	7. State:	8. Zip Code:

9. Mailing Address (street and number, post office box or rural route and box number):

10. City:	11. State:	12. Zip Code:

Type of Organization (Check only one)

☐ **American Legion**
(See item 78)

☐ **Biomedical Research Foundations**
(See item 1)

☐ **Boys & Girls Clubs of America Affiliate**
(See item 2)

☐ **Boy Scouts of America; Girl Scouts of U.S.A.; Camp Fire U.S.A. Council Organizations**
(See item 3)

☐ **Career Technology Student Organizations**
(See item 4)

☐ **Charitable Health Organizations**
(See item 5)

☐ **Children's Homes on Church-owned Property**
(See item 6)

☐ **Children's Homes Supported by Churches**
(See item 69)

☐ **Church**
(See item 7)

☐ **City or County Trust or Authority**
(See item 8)

☐ **Collection and Distribution**
(See item 9)

☐ **Community Blood Banks**
(See item 10)

☐ **Community Mental Health Center**
(See item 11)

☐ **Community-based Health Center**
(See item 12)

☐ **Community-based Autonomous Member**
(See item 13)

☐ **Construction Projects by Organizations Providing End-of-Life Care and Access to Hospice Services**
(See item 14)

☐ **Cultural Organization for Disadvantaged Children**
(See item 15)

☐ **Disabled American Veterans, Dept. of Oklahoma, Inc.**
(See item 16)

☐ **Federal Government or its Instrumentality**
(See item 19)

☐ **Fab Lab**
(See item 79)

☐ **Federally Chartered Credit Union**
(See item 20)

☐ **Health Center**
(See item 21)

☐ **Federally Recognized Indian Tribes**
(See item 22)

☐ **Grand River Dam Authority**
(See item 23)

☐ **Hazardous Waste Treatment Facility**
(See item 24)

☐ **Indigent Health Care Revolving Fund Clinic**
(See item 25)

☐ **Marine Corps League of Oklahoma [1356(78)] (SB 353-Effective July 1, 2018)**
(See item 76)

☐ **Meals on Wheels**
(See item 26)

☐ **Metropolitan Area Homeless Service Provider**
(See item 27)

☐ **Museums Accredited by the American Association of Museums**
(See item 29)

☐ **NRA/Other Organizations That Defend 2nd Amendment Rights**
(See item 30)

☐ **National Guard Association of Oklahoma [1356(77)] (SB 353-Effective July 1, 2018)**
(See instructions - Item 75)

☐ **National Volunteer Women's Service Organization**
(See item 31)

☐ **Non-accredited Museums**
(See item 83)

☐ **Nonprofit Corporation Rural Water District**
(See item 72)

☐ **Nonprofit Organizations that Construct, Remodel and Sell Affordable Housing**
(See item 81)

A

(Continued on page B)

Appendix 2.01. Oklahoma: Application for Sales Tax Exemption.

Type of Organization (Check only one)

- ☐ Nonprofit Organizations Restoring Single Family Housing Following a Disaster (See item 82)
- ☐ Oklahoma Coal Mining (See item 32)
- ☐ Older Americans Act (See item 33)
- ☐ On-site Universal Pre-Kindergarten Education (See item 34)
- ☐ Organizations for Rehabilitation of Court-adjudicated Juveniles (See item 35)
- ☐ Organizations for Educating Community Regarding the Developmentally Disabled (See item 36)
- ☐ Organizations Funding Scholarships in the Medical Field. (See item 37)
- ☐ Organizations Operating As Collaborative Models Connecting Community Agencies In One Location (See item 74)
- ☐ Organizations Providing Education Relating to Robotics (See item 67)
- ☐ Organizations Supporting State Parks in Oklahoma (See item 64)

- ☐ Parent-Teacher Associations or Organizations (See item 38)
- ☐ Preservation of Wetlands and Habitat for Wild Ducks (See item 39)
- ☐ Preservation and Conservation of Wild Turkeys (See item 40)
- ☐ Private Schools-Elementary/ Secondary (See item 41)
- ☐ Private School-Higher Education (See item 42)
- ☐ Public School Districts (See item 43)
- ☐ Public Schools of Higher Education (See item 44)
- ☐ Qualified Neighborhood Watch Organizations (See item 45)
- ☐ Rural Electric Cooperative (See item 47)
- ☐ Public Nonprofit Rural Water District (See item 48)
- ☐ Sales of Commercial Forestry Service Equipment (See item 84)
- ☐ School Foundations (See item 17)

- ☐ Shelter for Abused, Neglected or Abandoned Children (See item 49)
- ☐ Spaceport User (See item 68)
- ☐ State of Oklahoma, Local or County Government Entity (See item 50)
- ☐ Veterans of Foreign Wars of United States, Oklahoma Chapters (See item 51)
- ☐ Veterans' organizations that financially support area veteran's organizations for constructing a memorial or museum (See Item 77)
- ☐ Volunteer Fire Department-Title 18 (See item 52)
- ☐ Youth Athletic Teams (See item 66)
- ☐ Youth Camps (See item 54)
- ☐ YWCA OR YMCA (See item 55)

Additional documentation may be required.

13. This is to certify that the organization and responsible person(s) listed understand that only purchases of items for use solely by the organization are exempt from sales tax. Exemptions issued by this application will be properly utilized and safeguarded from abuse.

Signature of Authorized Representative (If a corporation or LLC, should be an officer or member)　**14.** Name (Printed) of Authorized Representative

15. Title of Authorized Representative　　　**16.** Date

Mandatory inclusion of Social Security and/or Federal Identification numbers is required on forms filed with the Oklahoma Tax Commission (OTC) pursuant to Title 68 of the Oklahoma Statutes and Regulations thereunder, for identification purposes, and are deemed part of the confidential files and records of the OTC. Your federal identification number does <u>not</u> qualify you for the sales tax exemption.

Note: All exempt purchases must be invoiced to the organization and paid by funds or check directly from the organization to qualify for the exemption.

Attach all required documents and mail to:　　**Oklahoma Tax Commission**
Oklahoma City, OK 73194

The Oklahoma Tax Commission is not required to give actual notice of changes in any state tax law.

B

Appendix 2.02: Oklahoma: Application for Sales Tax Exemption by Motion Picture or Television Production Companies

Form 13-88
Revised 11-2021

Application for Sales Tax Exemption
by Motion Picture or Television Production Companies
Oklahoma Tax Commission
Oklahoma City, OK 73194
(Print or Type All Information.)

1.	How is Business Owned:	☐ Individual	☐ Partnership	☐ Corporation	☐ Limited Liability

2. Name of Production Company:

3. Business Phone (Area code and number):

4. FEIN: ☐☐☐☐☐☐☐☐☐

5. Mailing Address: (Street and number, post office box or rural route and box number)

City   State   Zip Code

6. Name of Individual, Partners, Responsible Corporation Officer or Managing Members:

A Name (Last, First, Middle Initial)   Social Security Number   Title

Mailing Address   City, State and Zip Code

B Name (Last, First, Middle Initial)   Social Security Number   Title

Mailing Address   City, State and Zip Code

7. Location of Representative Responsible for Expenditure Records:

Address/Street Number or Directions (Do not use post office box or rural route)   City   State   Zip Code

8. Name and Phone Number of Person to Contact:

Name   Business Phone (Area code and number)

9. Projected Dates of Production Activities in Oklahoma: _____ through _____

10. Estimated Total Production Expenditures Subject to Sales and/or Use Tax: $_____

11. Name of Production: _____
(Check all that apply.)
A. Is the production a: ☐ Documentary   ☐ Special   ☐ Music Video   ☐ Television Commercial
☐ Television Program   ☐ Full Length Motion Picture

B. If a television program, will it serve as a: ☐ Pilot   ☐ Segment for a Series

C. Is the production being taped or filmed for: ☐ Theatrical Release   ☐ Network Release
☐ National Release   ☐ Regional Syndication

D. If no check is made in "C" above, is the production instead only to be shown via local media outlets?
☐ Yes   ☐ No

An individual, general partner, corporate officer or authorized representative must sign this application. The answers given and information provided above are true and correct to the best of my knowledge and belief.

12. Type or Print Name and Title

13. Signature   **14.** Date

Office Use

OTC Project Number

C

222

Appendix 2.03: Oklahoma: Application for 100 Percent Disabled Veteran Household Member Exemption Card

Form 13-55
Revised 11-2021

Oklahoma Tax Commission
Application for 100% Disabled Veteran
Household Member Exemption Card

Qualified 100% disabled veterans may obtain an additional exemption card for a household member* who is authorized to make purchases on their behalf.

Purchases made by or on behalf of the 100% disabled veteran qualified for the exemption are limited to $25,000.00 per year.

Qualified Veteran Requesting Additional Card:

Name: _____

Sales Tax Exemption Number: _____

Authorized Household Member*:

Name: _____

I, the undersigned veteran or authorized representative, declare under the penalties of perjury that I have examined this application and to the best of my knowledge the facts set forth are true and correct. If signed by a person other than the veteran, Form BT-129 Power of Attorney must be attached.

_____   _____
Signature of Surviving Spouse or Authorized Representative   Contact Phone Number

Date: _____

Mail to: **Oklahoma Tax Commission**
            Oklahoma City, OK 73194

*An authorized household member includes a qualified veteran's spouse or other person residing with the qualified veteran.

D

Appendix 2.04: Oklahoma: Application for Surviving Spouse of a 100 Percent Disabled Veteran Household Member Exemption Card

Form 13-55-A
Revised 11-2021

Oklahoma Tax Commission
Application for Surviving Spouse of a 100% Disabled Veteran Household Member Exemption Card

A qualified surviving spouse of a 100% disabled veteran may obtain an additional exemption card for a household member* who is authorized to make purchases on their behalf.

Purchases made by or on behalf of the surviving spouse of a 100% disabled veteran qualified for the exemption are limited to $1,000.00 per year.

Qualified Surviving Spouse Requesting Additional Card:

Name: _____

Sales Tax Exemption Number: _____

Authorized Household Member*:

Name: _____

I, the undersigned surviving spouse or authorized representative, declare under the penalties of perjury that I have examined this application and to the best of my knowledge the facts set forth are true and correct. If signed by a person other than the surviving spouse, Form BT-129 Power of Attorney must be attached.

_____   _____

Signature of Surviving Spouse or Authorized Representative   Contact Phone Number

Date: _____

Mail to: **Oklahoma Tax Commission**
               Oklahoma City, OK 73194

*An authorized household member must reside with the eligible person and be authorized to make purchases on the eligible person's behalf.

E

Appendix 2.05: Oklahoma: Application for Sales/Use Tax Exemption for Volunteer Fire Departments

Form 13-36
Revised 11-2021

Application for Sales/Use Tax Exemption
for Volunteer Fire Departments
Organized under Title 18 Section 592 of the Oklahoma Statutes

Federal Employer Identification Number (FEIN)	Business Phone (Area Code and Number)	OFFICE USE ONLY

☐☐ – ☐☐☐☐☐☐☐   (____) ____ – _____

OFFICE USE ONLY

Exemption Number
☐☐☐☐☐☐

☐ Approved

☐ Denied

Organization Information (Please Print)

_____
Legal Name of Volunteer Fire Organization as Registered with Oklahoma Secretary of State

SIC Code
| 1 | 7 | 3 | 8 | 9 |

_____
Organization Physical Location (Provide address or directions, Do not use post office box or rural route number.)

NAICS Code
| 9 | 2 | 2 | 1 | 6 | 0 |

_____
City   State   Zip Code

Exemption Year
☐☐

_____
Mailing Address (Address, post office box or rural route and box number)

COPO
☐☐☐☐

_____
City   State   Zip Code

Title 68 Section 1356.1 of the Oklahoma Statutes
Added by Laws 1991, c. 208, § 2, effective July 1, 1991; Amended by Laws 2004, SB 1121, c. 535 § 7, effective November 1, 2004.

(A) In order to qualify for any exemption authorized by paragraph 17 of Section 1356 of this title, at the time of sale, the person to whom the sale is made may be required to furnish the vendor proof of eligibility for such exemption as required by this section.

(B) All vendors shall honor the proof of eligibility for sales tax exemption as authorized by this section and sales to a person providing such proof shall be exempt from the tax levied by this article.

(C) A fire department organized pursuant to Section 592 of Title 18 of the Oklahoma Statutes may obtain one card, the size and design of which shall be prescribed by the Oklahoma Tax Commission, which shall constitute proof of eligibility for sales tax exemptions authorized by paragraph 17 of Section 1356 of this title. Such card may be obtained upon application to the Tax Commission on a form prescribed by the Tax Commission. The application shall contain such other information as may be required by the Tax Commission. Upon approval by the Tax Commission, the fire department shall be issued one card as prescribed by this section. The card shall be renewable every three (3) years upon application therefor, as provided by this section, to the Tax Commission.

This is to certify that the organization and responsible person(s) understand that purchases of items for use solely by the organization are exempt from sales tax. Exemptions issued by this application will be properly utilized and safeguarded from abuse.

_____
Signature of Fire Chief   Date

Mandatory inclusion of Social Security Number and/or Federal Identification Number is required on forms filed with the Oklahoma Tax Commission (OTC) pursuant to Title 68 of the Oklahoma Statutes and regulations thereunder for identification purposes, and are deemed part of the confidential files and records of the OTC.

The OTC is not required to give actual notice of changes in any state tax law.

Oklahoma Tax Commission
Oklahoma City, OK 73194

Appendix 2.06: New Mexico: Application for Nontaxable Transaction Certificates

ACD-31050
Rev. 04/23/2020

New Mexico Taxation and Revenue Department
APPLICATION FOR NONTAXABLE TRANSACTION CERTIFICATES

REQUIREMENTS: All New Mexico buyers/lessees who wish to execute Nontaxable Transaction Certificates (NTTCs) are required to register with the Taxation and Revenue Department using Form ACD-31015, Application for Business Tax Identification Number. Once the registration process has been completed and a New Mexico business tax identification number (CRS number) has been issued for your business you can complete the Application for Nontaxable Transaction Certificates below and submit it to your closest district office.

CAUTION: Fraudulent statements made to obtain certificates, or fraudulent use of certificates received pursuant to this application with intent to evade or defeat the tax may subject the person or business to a fine of not more than ten thousand dollars ($10,000) or imprisonment for not more than five (5) years or both (Sections 7-1-72 NMSA 1978 and 7-1-73 NMSA 1978).

NTTC DESCRIPTIONS AND AUTHORIZED USES: See reverse for complete descriptions of NTTC types.
- Type 2: for tangibles for resale, lease or re-lease, or for purchase by manufacturer.
- Type 5: for services for resale, for export, or for services performed on manufactured products.
- Type 6: for construction contractor's purchase of construction materials, construction services, construction-related services or for the lease of construction equipment
- Type 9: for purchase of tangible personal property by New Mexico or United States governments, 501(c)(3) organization, or credit unions
- Type 10: for purchase or lease of tangible personal property or services by a person who holds an interest in a qualified generating facility
- Type 11: for purchase of tangible personal property that is consumed in the manufacturing process[1]
- Type 12: for purchase of utilities that are consumed in the manufacturing process[1]
- Type 15: for tangible personal property purchased by qualified federal contractors
- Type 16: for sales of property, services and leases to qualified film production companies, accredited foreign missions, and their accredited members
- Type 17: for government agencies' or 501(c)(3) organizations' purchases of construction material that is tangible personal property[1]
- Type OSB NTTCs are issued to registered New Mexico sellers/lessors to execute to Out-of-State Buyers who are not registered with the Department, but who will resell tangible personal property outside of New Mexico

[1] **To request the Type 11, 12 and 17 NTTCs: Please submit below specified forms:**
- Type 11: Requires Form RPD-41378, Application for Type 11 or 12 Nontaxable Certificates
- Type 12: Requires Form RPD-41378, Application for Type 11 or 12 Nontaxable Certificates and RPD-41377, Manufacturing Agreement to Pay Gross Receipts on Behalf of a Utility Company for Certain Utility Sales
- Type 17: Requires Form RPD-41250, Application for Type 17 Nontaxable Transaction Certificates and ACD-31050, Application for Nontaxable Transaction Certificates

Above forms are available online www.tax.newmexico.gov or from your local district office.

Taxpayer Access Point (TAP) for NTTCs: The Department encourages all taxpayers to use TAP to apply for, execute, record, print and request additional NTTCs online. If you know the seller's/lessor's CRS identification number to whom you wish to execute a NTTC, you may immediately execute the NTTC online. When the recipient's CRS identification number is known, there is no limit to executing NTTCs on TAP, but you may request up to five (5) NTTCs to be executed at a later date if the seller's/lessor's name and CRS identification number is not known. You must first record executed NTTC information before applying for additional NTTCs to be executed at a later date. Please note that on the TAP system third parties (e.g., CPAs, accountants, bookkeepers, etc.) cannot request or execute NTTC's on behalf of their clients/employers. For instructions on how to obtain NTTCs online, go to https://tap.state.nm.us. IF YOU DO NOT HAVE INTERNET ACCESS COMPLETE THE APPLICATION FORM PROVIDED BELOW

HOW TO APPLY OR REORDER: If you do not yet have the name and CRS identification number of the vendor to whom you wish to execute the NTTC, complete the application below, providing all information requested. Mail the application to the New Mexico Taxation and Revenue Department, P.O. Box 5557, Santa Fe, New Mexico 87502-5557, or you may deliver it to your local district office.

NOTE: You may reorder additional NTTCs ONLY after your executed NTTCs have been recorded with the Department. To record your executed NTTCs, submit the Nontaxable Transaction Certificate Report or record them online. The Department will only issue a maximum of five (5) NTTCs to be executed at a later date.

APPLICATION FOR NONTAXABLE TRANSACTION CERTIFICATES
To be executed at a later date (All information below must be completed)

BUSINESS INFORMATION OF APPLICANT

NM CRS IDENTIFICATION NUMBER OF APPLICANT

Name: _____

Mailing Address: _____

City: _____ State: _____ Zip: _____

Date: _____ Phone No: _____

Print Name: _____

Authorized Signature: _____

0 _ _ - _ _ _ _ _ _ _ - 0 0 - _

☐ New Application

☐ Reorder

Type of NTTC

CONTRACTORS LICENSE NUMBER
(If applicable)

____ ____ ____ ____

Quantity Requested: 5 combined maximum
(circle number)

	1	2	3	4	5
	1	2	3	4	5

New Mexico Taxation and Revenue Department, PO Box 5557, Santa Fe, New Mexico 87502-5557

Appendix 3

Tax Reporting Forms

The forms included here are intended to demonstrate and compare the different designs of the forms that may be used when completing sales tax returns. Following are copies of the printed version. The versions available on a tax entity's website will likely be different from these.

Note: The forms included may not be the latest versions.

Appendix number	State	Form number	Form title and comments
3.01	Texas	01-117	Texas Sales and Use Tax Return—Short Form
3.02	Texas	01-114	Texas Sales and Use Tax Return
3.03	Texas	01-115	Texas Sales and Use Tax Return—Outlet Supplement
3.04	Texas	01-118	Texas Sales and Use Tax Prepayment Report
3.05	Texas	00-985	Assignment of Right to Refund
3.06	Texas	00-957	Texas Claim for Refund
3.07	Texas	01-148	Texas Sales and Use Tax Return Credits and Customs Broker Schedule

Appendix 3.01. Texas: Sales and Use Tax Return—Short Form

 01-117
(Rev.5-19/39)

Texas Sales and Use Tax Return - *Short Form*

Who May File the Short Form - You may file the short form if you meet **all** of the following criteria:

* your business has a single location in Texas;
* you report applicable local taxes only to the entities (city, transit authority, county or special purpose district) in which your business is located;
* you do not prepay your state and local taxes;
* you do not have a credit, including bad debt credit, to reduce your tax due on this return;
* you do not have customs broker refunds to report; and
* you are not a remote seller or marketplace provider.

You must file the long form (Form 01-114) if any of these statements do not apply to your business. You must file a long form if you are responsible for out-of-state use tax and have no in-state locations.

If you have a credit for taxes you paid or customs broker refunds to report, you are required to complete Form 01-114 Sales and Use Tax Return and Form 01-148 Texas Sales and Use Tax Return Credits and Customs Broker Schedule. If you are claiming bad debt credit, you must file electronically at https://comptroller.texas.gov/taxes/file-pay/.

When to File - Returns must be filed or postmarked on or before the 20th day of the month following the end of each reporting period. If the due date falls on a Saturday, Sunday or legal holiday, the next business day will be the due date.

Business Changes - If you are out of business or if your mailing or outlet address has changed, you can make these changes online at www.comptroller.texas.gov/taxes/sales/, "Registering and Reporting Texas Sales and Use Tax," or blacken the box to the right of the signature line on this return. If you are a Remote Seller, use form 01-798, Remote Sellers Intent to Terminate Use Tax Responsibilities, to end your tax responsibility.

Instructions for Filing an Amended Texas Sales and Use Tax Return - You may file an amended return on paper or electronically via Webfile or Electronic Data Interchange (EDI). Additional documentation may be required to validate your request. If you choose to file a paper amended return please follow these steps:
1. Make a copy of the original return you filed or download a blank return from our website at www.comptroller.texas.gov/taxes/forms/.
2. Write "AMENDED RETURN" on the top of the form.
3. If you're using a copy of your original return, cross out the amounts that are wrong and write in the correct amounts. If you're using a blank return, enter the amounts as they should have appeared on the original return.
4. Sign and date the return.

If the amended return shows you *underpaid* your taxes, please send the additional tax due plus any penalties and interest that may apply.

If the amended return shows you *overpaid* your taxes and you are requesting a refund, you must meet all of the requirements for a refund claim. Refer to *Sales Tax Refunds* on the Comptroller's website at www.comptroller.texas.gov/taxes/sales/refunds/.

Whom to Contact for Assistance - If you have any questions regarding sales tax, you may contact the Texas State Comptroller's field office in your area or call 800-252-5555.

General Instructions

* Please do not write in shaded areas.
* If any preprinted information on this return is incorrect, OR if you do not qualify to file this return, contact the Comptroller's office.
* Do not leave Items 1, 2, 3 or 4 blank. Enter "0" if the amount is zero.
* You must file a return even if you had no sales.
* If any amounts entered are negative, bracket them as follows: <xx,xxx.xx>.

* If *hand printing*, please enter all numbers within the boxes, as shown. Use black ink.

    0 1 2 3 4 5 6 7 8 9

* If *typing*, numbers may be typed consecutively.

    0123456789

▼ ▼ ▼ ▼ ▼ ▼ ▼ ▼ ▼ ▼ ▼ ▼ **PLEASE DETACH AND RETURN BOTTOM PORTION ONLY** ▼ ▼ ▼ ▼ ▼ ▼ ▼ ▼ ▼ ▼ ▼ ▼

01-117 (Rev.5-19/39)
TEXAS SALES AND USE TAX RETURN HHH

a. 26140 • Do not fold, staple or paper clip • Write only in white areas.

c. ■ Taxpayer number

d. Filing period

g. Due date

f. Outlet no./location ■

k. Outlet address *(Do not use a P.O. box address)*

Taxpayer name and mailing address

L. OUT OF BUSINESS DATE DO NOT ENTER UNLESS ▼ no longer in business. ▼

*** INTERNET ***

1. TOTAL TEXAS SALES
   ■ *(Whole dollars only)* .00
2. TAXABLE SALES
   ■ *(Whole dollars only)* .00
3. TAXABLE PURCHASES +
   ■ *(Whole dollars only)* .00
4. Total amount subject to tax =
   ■ *(Item 2 plus Item 3)* .00
5. Tax due - *Multiply Item 4 by the combined tax rate (Include state & local)*
6. Timely filing discount (0.005) −
7. Prior payments −
8. Net tax due =
   (Subtract Items 6 and 7 from Item 5.)
9. Penalty & interest +
   (See instructions.)
10. TOTAL AMOUNT DUE AND PAYABLE =
    ■ *(Item 8 plus Item 9.)*

I declare that the information in this document and any attachments is true and correct to the best of my knowledge and belief.

sign here ▶ Taxpayer or duly authorized agent

Date   Daytime phone *(Area code & no.)*

Blacken this box ▶ if out of business or address has changed.

Appendix 3.02. Texas: Sales and Use Tax Return

Appendix 3.03. Texas: Texas Sales and Use Tax Return—Outlet Supplement

01-115
(Rev.4-19/25)

TEXAS SALES AND USE TAX RETURN
- OUTLET SUPPLEMENT -

EEEE

b. ■

*** INTERNET *** Page of

a. ■ 26100   c. Taxpayer number ■

d. Filing period

e. ■

Make any necessary changes next to the incorrect information for any location. *(Do not use P.O. box addresses.)*

f. Taxpayer name

SALES TAX QUESTIONS? CALL US! 1-800-252-5555

g. Due date

• *Do not staple or paper clip.*

PLEASE PRINT YOUR NUMERALS LIKE THIS

0 1 2 3 4 5 6 7 8 9

---

1. TOTAL TEXAS SALES
(Whole dollars only) ■

2. TAXABLE SALES
(Whole dollars only) ■

3. TAXABLE PURCHASES
(Whole dollars only) ■

4. Amount subject to state tax
(Item 2 plus Item 3) ■

5. Amount subject to local tax
(Amount for city, transit, county and SPD must be equal.) ■

6. Physical location (outlet) name and address
(Do not use a P.O. box address.)   Outlet no. ■

7. AMOUNT OF TAX DUE FOR THIS OUTLET *(Dollars and cents)*
(Multiply "Amount subject to tax" by "TAX RATE" for state and local tax due)
TAX RATES

X   .062500   =   7a.State tax *(include in Item 8a)*

X   =   7b.Local tax *(include in Item 8b)*

---

1. TOTAL TEXAS SALES
(Whole dollars only) ■

2. TAXABLE SALES
(Whole dollars only) ■

3. TAXABLE PURCHASES
(Whole dollars only) ■

4. Amount subject to state tax
(Item 2 plus Item 3) ■

5. Amount subject to local tax
(Amount for city, transit, county and SPD must be equal.) ■

6. Physical location (outlet) name and address
(Do not use a P.O. box address.)   Outlet no. ■

7. AMOUNT OF TAX DUE FOR THIS OUTLET *(Dollars and cents)*
(Multiply "Amount subject to tax" by "TAX RATE" for state and local tax due)
TAX RATES

X   .062500   =   7a.State tax *(include in Item 8a)*

X   =   7b.Local tax *(include in Item 8b)*

---

1. TOTAL TEXAS SALES
(Whole dollars only) ■

2. TAXABLE SALES
(Whole dollars only) ■

3. TAXABLE PURCHASES
(Whole dollars only) ■

4. Amount subject to state tax
(Item 2 plus Item 3) ■

5. Amount subject to local tax
(Amount for city, transit, county and SPD must be equal.) ■

6. Physical location (outlet) name and address
(Do not use a P.O. box address.)   Outlet no. ■

7. AMOUNT OF TAX DUE FOR THIS OUTLET *(Dollars and cents)*
(Multiply "Amount subject to tax" by "TAX RATE" for state and local tax due)
TAX RATES

X   .062500   =   7a.State tax *(include in Item 8a)*

X   =   7b.Local tax *(include in Item 8b)*

---

1. TOTAL TEXAS SALES
(Whole dollars only) ■

2. TAXABLE SALES
(Whole dollars only) ■

3. TAXABLE PURCHASES
(Whole dollars only) ■

4. Amount subject to state tax
(Item 2 plus Item 3) ■

5. Amount subject to local tax
(Amount for city, transit, county and SPD must be equal.) ■

6. Physical location (outlet) name and address
(Do not use a P.O. box address.)   Outlet no. ■

7. AMOUNT OF TAX DUE FOR THIS OUTLET *(Dollars and cents)*
(Multiply "Amount subject to tax" by "TAX RATE" for state and local tax due)
TAX RATES

X   .062500   =   7a.State tax *(include in Item 8a)*

X   =   7b.Local tax *(include in Item 8b)*

TOTAL TAX DUE ON THIS PAGE (For Taxpayer Use Only)	STATE TAX	LOCAL TAX

You have certain rights under Ch. 559, Government Code, to review, request and correct information we have on file about you. Contact us at the address or phone number listed in the instructions.

Appendix 3.04. Texas: Sales and Use Tax Prepayment Report

01-118
(Rev.5-19/18)

TEXAS SALES AND USE TAX PREPAYMENT REPORT

a. Taxpayer name	b. Taxpayer number
c. Period ending	d. Date due

COMPUTATION OF ESTIMATED TAX DUE (Compute TAX DUE by multiplying AMOUNT SUBJECT TO TAX by TAX RATE)	ESTIMATED AMOUNT SUBJECT TO TAX (Report in whole dollars)	TAX RATE	ESTIMATED TAX DUE (Multiply estimated amount by tax rate)
1. State tax _____	.00	X (6 1/4%) .062500 =	1a.
2. Local tax _____	.00	X (2%) .020000 =	2a.
Local tax _____	.00	X (1 7/8%) .018750 =	2b.
Local tax _____	.00	X (1 3/4%) .017500 =	2c.
Local tax _____	.00	X (1 5/8%) .016250 =	2d.
Local tax _____	.00	X (1 1/2%) .015000 =	2e.
Local tax _____	.00	X (1 3/8%) .013750 =	2f.
Local tax _____	.00	X (1 1/4%) .012500 =	2g.
Local tax _____	.00	X (1 1/8%) .011250 =	2h.
Local tax _____	.00	X (1%) .010000 =	2i.
Local tax _____	.00	X (7/8%) .008750 =	2j.
Local tax _____	.00	X (3/4%) .007500 =	2k.
Local tax _____	.00	X (5/8%) .006250 =	2l.
Local tax _____	.00	X (1/2%) .005000 =	2m.
Local tax _____	.00	X (3/8%) .003750 =	2n.
Local tax _____	.00	X (1/4%) .002500 =	2o.
Local tax _____	.00	X (1/8%) .001250 =	2p.

COMPUTATION OF PREPAYMENT	STATE TAX	LOCAL TAX
	(From Item 1a)	(Total of Items 2a through 2p)
3. Total estimated tax due for this filing period _____		
4. Prepayment discount rate _____	(1 3/4%) .01750	(1 3/4%) .01750
5. Prepayment discount (Multiply Item 3 by Item 4) _____		
	6a. (Enter here and in Item 8.)	6b. (Enter here and in Item 9.)
6. Prepayment amount (Item 3 minus Item 5) _____		

7. TOTAL AMOUNT OF PREPAYMENT (Total of Items 6a and 6b) _____

▲ DETACH HERE AND RETURN WITH YOUR PAYMENT. ▲

Form 01-118
(Rev.5-19/18)
**TEXAS SALES AND USE
TAX PREPAYMENT**
• Do not fold, staple or paper clip

JJJJ   e. ■

*** INTERNET ***

f. Taxpayer number	g. Due date
h. Filing period	i.

I declare that the information in this document and any attachments is true and correct to the best of my knowledge and belief.

sign here ▶ Taxpayer or duly authorized agent

Daytime phone (Area code & no.)	Date

j. Taxpayer name and mailing address (Make any necessary name or address changes below.)

8. State prepayment
(From Item 6a)
■ 02 _____ ■

9. Local prepayment
(From Item 6b)
■ 04 _____ ■

10. TOTAL PREPAYMENT
(Total of Items 8 & 9) _____ $

Make amount in Item 10 payable to:
STATE COMPTROLLER
Our mailing address is:
P.O. Box 149354
Austin, TX 78714-9354

k.

■ T Code   ■ Taxpayer number   ■ Period

26050

Appendix 3.05. Texas: Assignment of Right to Refund

ASSIGNMENT OF RIGHT TO REFUND

To the Comptroller of Public Accounts for the State of Texas (hereinafter "Comptroller"):

(1) My name is _____ , and I am a duly authorized representative of _____ (the "Assignor"). By executing this Assignment of Right to a Refund ("Assignment"), the Assignor assigns all rights and interest to the tax refund herein described that the Assignor may have to _____ (the "Assignee"), subject to the limitation noted herein. The Assignee's Taxpayer Number is _____ (if permitted in Texas).

(2) Assignor hereby assigns the Assignee (check whichever is applicable):

_____ a. The right to file a request for a refund and to receive the refund.

_____ b. The right to receive the refund only.

(3) The tax refund that is the subject of this Assignment is described as follows:

Tax Type: _____

Period: _____

Transactions: _____

_____ (Attach schedule, if necessary.)

Other specific limitations: _____

(4) The Assignor understands that the Comptroller may require both parties to provide documents or information necessary for the Comptroller to verify the validity of the refund claim and/or to transfer any verified amount to the Assignee.

(5) By executing this Assignment, the Assignor affirms that the Assignor has neither previously claimed a refund nor taken a credit on a return for taxes that are subject of this Assignment, and further affirms that the Assignor will not claim a refund or a credit for those taxes in the future.

Executed _____ day of _____ , 20 ____ .

_____	_____
Assignor Entity Name	Assignor Taxpayer Number
_____	
Print or type the name of person authorizing assignment	
_____	
Relationship to entity (i.e., President, Treasurer)	
_____	_____
Signature of person authorizing assignment	Date
_____	
Area code/daytime phone number	

Form 00-985 (Rev.9-05/2)

Appendix 3.06. Texas: Claim for Refund

 00-957
(Rev.6-19/9)

Texas Claim for Refund

IMPORTANT: If the purchaser did not have an active Sales Tax permit during the claim period, the purchaser is required to obtain a completed and signed Texas Assignment of Right to Refund (Form 00-985) and submit it, along with this claim, to the Texas Comptroller's Office. However, if the purchaser is requesting a refund of local tax only, paid to a Remote Seller, the Texas Assignment of Right to Refund form is not required. If someone other than the taxpayer/claimant submits the claim, a completed **Power of Attorney (Form 01-137)** must be submitted.

For information on documentation required to file a **Sales Tax** refund claim, please visit our website at **www.comptroller.texas.gov/taxes/sales/refunds/**.

Taxpayer/Claimant name	Claimant ID number *(Texas taxpayer number if you have one)*
Mailing address *(Street)*	Total amount of refund requested:
City, state and ZIP code	☐ Check here if you entered an amended return online for this same period.

1. Period of claim .... First date: *(mm/dd/yy)* _____   Last date: *(mm/dd/yy)* _____

2. Please state fully, and in detail, each reason or ground on which this refund claim is founded. Please note, simply stating "Tax paid in error" does not provide a sufficient reason for a refund. *Attach additional sheets, if necessary.*

_____

_____

_____

_____

3. Type of tax or fee upon which this refund claim is based *(Enter code from list below.)* .... _____

26 - Sales Tax	**50** - Texas Emissions Reduction Surcharge	**64** - Petroleum Product Delivery Fee	**73** - Mixed Beverage Gross Receipt
27 - Direct Pay	**63** - Mixed Beverage Sales	**70** - Motor Vehicle Seller-Financed Sales	**75** - Hotel Occupancy - State Only

Other tax _____

4. **For Accounting Errors** - submit accounting records. **For other claims:** Submit invoices for each claim request. Attach a schedule *(see example Form 01-911)* to support claims with more than 10 sales invoices.

5. FOR SALES TAX ONLY, the name, authority ID, and amount of tax claimed for each local jurisdiction must be included on the schedule Form 01-911. *(To find local codes go to* **https://mycpa.cpa.state.tx.us/atj/** *or ask the seller.)*

Name of contact *(please print)*	Email address of contact:		
sign here ▶ Signature of taxpayer/claimant/contact:		Date	Daytime phone *(Area code and number)*

You have certain rights under Chapters 552 and 559, Government Code, to review, request and correct information we have on file about you. Contact us at the address or phone number listed below.

Please choose one method of submitting your request and supporting documentation:

Mail to: Comptroller of Public Accounts Revenue Accounting Division Sales & Motor Vehicle Tax Refunds 111 E. 17th Street Austin, TX 78774-0100	Email to: refund.request@cpa.texas.gov Inquiries only: refund.status@cpa.texas.gov	For assistance, call 1-800-531-5441 ext. 34545 or 512-463-4545.

Appendix 3.07. Texas: Sales and Use Tax Return—Credits and Customs Broker Schedule

* * * INTERNET * * *

01-148 (Rev.5-19/9)   HHHH

b.

a. ■ 26160 original

Page _____ of _____

Texas Sales and Use Tax Return
Credits and Customs Broker Schedule

c. Taxpayer number	d. Filing period	e.	f. Due date
■		■	

g. ___ Taxpayer name and mailing address *(Make corrections next to any incorrect information.)* ___

• *Do not staple or paper clip.*

• *Do not write in shaded areas.*

h. ■   i. ■

PLEASE PRINT YOUR NUMERALS LIKE THIS
0 1 2 3 4 5 6 7 8 9

If you are taking bad debt credit on your return, you must file electronically at https://comptroller.texas.gov/taxes/file-pay/. Bad debt is any portion of the sales price of a taxable item that a retailer or a private label credit provider cannot collect. The bad debt must be taken as a deduction on the federal income tax return during the same or subsequent reporting period.

Examples of Credits on Purchases include paying or accruing tax on a non-taxable or exempt purchase in error, such as resale or manufacturing exemptions, or accrued and paid tax on the same taxable purchase.

Examples of Credits on Sales include remitting tax on sales that qualify for an exemption such as resale, manufacturing, agricultural/timber, or remitting tax on sales where merchandise is returned.

Other credits include calculation or bookkeeping errors.

If you are claiming bad debt credit to reduce your tax due, you must file electronically at www.comptroller.texas.gov/taxes/file-pay/.

Claim the credit in Item 2 by subtracting the sum of purchases and/or sales you paid taxes on in error, or refunded to a customer, from the amount of taxable sales.

Credit for a local taxing jurisdiction cannot be taken unless you have reported that jurisdiction on a previously filed tax return. A claim for refund must be filed directly with the Comptroller. Refund instructions are available at www.comptroller.texas.gov/taxes/sales/refunds.

Credits For Tax Paid - *If you answered "YES," to Item j of your Sales Tax Report, Form 01-114, you must complete Items 1 and 2, below.*

NOTE: The data entered here is for information purposes only. It is not used in calculating tax due on this report.

1. Amount of tax credit being taken on this return
   (Enter dollars and cents.) _____ ■

2. Earliest date of the tax paid in error for this credit
   (mm-dd-yy) _____ ■

Customs Broker Refunds - *If you answered "YES," to Item k of your Sales Tax Report, Form 01-114, you must complete Item 3, below.*

NOTE: The data entered here is for information purposes only. It is not used in calculating tax due on this report.

3. *Enter the total state and local sales tax refunded for items exported outside the United States from all Texas Licensed Customs Broker Export Certificates (Enter dollars and cents.)* _____ ■

I declare that the information in this document and any attachments is true and correct to the best of my knowledge.

sign here ▶ | Taxpayer or duly authorized agent | Date | Daytime phone *(Area code & number)*

If you have any questions, call 1-800-252-5555.
Details are also available online at www.comptroller.texas.gov.

Mail to Comptroller of Public Accounts
P.O. Box 149354
Austin, TX 78714-9354

You have certain rights under Chapters 552 and 559, Government Code, to review, request and correct information we have on file about you. Contact us at the address or phone number listed on this form.

About the Author

Esther E. Carranza earned three bachelor degrees from the University of Saint Thomas in Houston, Texas: management information systems, economics, and business administration. She was first introduced to transactional taxes at the age of nineteen, when she was asked to work on a special project to help a company through a sales tax audit. Here is where her interest in transactional taxes started and grew.

Throughout her career, Esther has combined her knowledge and experience with information systems, accounting software, and taxes to help companies establish or improve their policies and procedures related to transactional taxes. She has worked with different aspects of transactional taxes, including procurement/buying, sales, accounting, auditing, tax reporting, and tax compliance.

Esther enjoys using her skills and knowledge to help people understand taxation and how it impacts their business. She is hoping that people will use the information found in *Basics about Sales, Use, and Other Transactional Taxes* to minimize their tax costs, improve their business processes, and increase their level of tax compliance.

Index